Flax

to

Freedom

Charles Germaine was a fugitive from
La Tremblade Prison in 1687.

—Vincent Family, *Descendants of Adrian Vincent*

6/30/10

To Dr Kaufman —
with thanks and
appreciation for all
your care —
Barbara

Flax
to
Freedom

Barbara Knickerbocker Beskind

Barbara Knickerbocker

BKB Press
New London, New Hampshire

Flax to Freedom
by Barbara Knickerbocker

Text © 2009 Barbara Knickerbocker Beskind
Artwork © 2008 Barbara Knickerbocker Beskind

BKB Press
103 Hilltop Place
New London NH 03257

If you wish to buy additional copies of *Flax to Freedom*,
contact the publisher.

ISBN 978-0-9817768-3-5

Flax to Freedom

is

dedicated

to

Charles Germaine,

an ancestor of mine,

who fled the iron chains

of

La Tremblade Prison

in

1687.

Acknowledgments

The church at the Historic Huguenot Street in New Paltz, New York provided a mental image for my drawing of the simple, square Huguenot church back in La Rochelle, France. The single entrance to this church opened to the north; according to my research, this had been their custom.

The Shaker Museum's Great Stone Building in Enfield, New Hampshire provided the image I used to portray the sturdy, stark harshness of the prison at La Tremblade, France.

I want to acknowledge the tutelage of Ann Compton of Woodstock, Vermont during the early stages of this book that has morphed from a chapter book for pre-teens to its present, expanded form for general readership. The characters experience subtle, deep feelings that are of greater interest to the adult reader. However, the context provides a fast-moving story of the history, the conflicts and a rich sociological account of life in rural France in the 1600s. With this in mind, I asked the following 7th graders to review the material for its suitability for them. Katie Scheuch and Jonalyn Burt of the New London Middle School, New London, New Hampshire and John Wilson, home-schooled in Lebanon, New Hampshire responded in the affirmative. I thank them for their time and constructive contributions.

I want to thank Erna Laing of Litchfield, New Hampshire for her review of the use of nautical terms and to Brad Sackett of Pike, New Hampshire and Charles Sackett Jr. of Warren, New Hampshire for their review of this as well as material relevant to the behavior of a donkey, an unlikely transitional feature in this story.

I also want to acknowledge Jean Winchester Kleinhomer's review of this material from the point of view of family history. In addition, I want to extend my appreciation to Sally Allen of Springfield, New Hampshire for her insightful suggestions about the content as she edited the manuscript.

I wish to express my deep thanks to Kitty Werner of RSB Press, Waitsfield, Vermont for her final editing and expertise as the designer of this book and its cover.

Preface

Flax to Freedom is the third book in a series of "windows on history." The early manuscript originated as a chapter-book during a course I took in 1996 with Ann Compton that was sponsored by the AVA Gallery of Lebanon, New Hampshire. It focused on writing, illustrating, and designing books for children.

This course took place before I had any interest in studying art. The instructor saw me primarily as a writer, thus excusing me from the art requirement. She suggested, instead, that I engage an illustrator for my work.

The week prior to the last class, I sketched out these cubistic illustrations almost as a lark, intended simply to indicate to an illustrator "what" and "where" certain drawings would be inserted within the narrative. I was as surprised as anyone in the class at this outcome. Here they are — just as they were drawn, with ink and watercolor pencils. This accounts for the unique shading of the black and white drawings in this edition.

Several years later I began a three-year study of art at the Sharon Art Center in Sharon, New Hampshire. I found abstract art and its early origins in Pre-Revolutionary Russia, intrigued me most.

Powder Keg, the first book in this series of "windows on history," is an historical autobiography that introduces two other ancestors and traces their origins in Europe at the time of the Protestant Reformation.

Touches of Life in Time and Space, the second "window on history" followed. Both were published in 2008. Each of these is also suitable for adolescent as well as adult readership and provides young people a rich contextual vocabulary.

Touches of Life in Time and Space is comprised of a series of historical poems starting with Henry Hudson. Other poems focus on family and life experience, to include the intense interest I found in art of the Russian Avant-garde (1910–1922). The 40 poems of this book are accompanied by more than 50 pieces of original art.

A fourth book, also a "window on history," is in preparation. It is entitled *Touches of Art and the Impact of the Russian Avant-garde*. It expands on the section of poetry on this subject from the book mentioned above. The book-in-process concerns my deep interest in the history and little-known early development of abstract art in Russia that was obscured under Stalin. Following Gorbachev's Glasnost in 1985, these pieces were brought out of hiding in 1987. Survival of it may again be at risk.

Historical Note

2009 marks the 500th Anniversary of the birth of John Calvin. Earliest followers of the 1500s were the French Huguenots, followed by the Walloon Reformists of the Belgic Lands.

In The Netherlands, they were called the Dutch Reformed and in Scotland they were Presbyterians. In America, the more recently-named Christian Reformed denomination is also a Calvinist church.

Introduction

Flax to Freedom is a fictionalized account surrounding factual information of a Huguenot ancestor. During my childhood I often heard the story of his escape from persecution in France.

Direct lineage of Charles Germaine through my maternal grandfather, Eugene Ham, is documented on page 130.

What intrigued me as a child, was to hear that Grandpa never wanted to sleep in a bed that did not allow his head to point north. As I have begun to unravel the historical background to this story, I feel it is possible this firmly entrenched trait may stem from early Huguenot customs, handed down through the generations.

What is also curious is the childhood memory of a very large, perfectly shaped conch shell at my grandparents' home in Verbank, New York.

This impressive conch shell had a glossy pink interior surface and was always placed in a revered spot beside the heavy, oak front door. As youngsters we were cautioned not to drop it as we held it close to our ears, intrigued by the sound we were told was the ocean's "roar."

How, or why, my grandparents happened to have this beautiful conch shell is unknown. It is unlikely that it ever had a direct connection to the role of the conch shell that was crucial to the survival of the early Huguenot communities. Now it makes me wonder.

The underlying theme of much of the writing in *Flax to Freedom* and *Powder Keg* is one of social and religious tolerance, one individual at a time. Both offer a point of view that would be a useful reference in middle school and high school libraries, Sunday School curricula, Christian Charter schools and home-schooling programs. Also depicted in *Powder Keg* is the little-known history shared between the first settlers of New Amsterdam who were Christians and the original Jews in North America who arrived in 1654.

Flax to Freedom

It is the **flax**

> that's grown in fields
> that's pulled in clumps
> that's retted in pools
> that's cracked to open
> that frees the strands
>> — **for spinning.**

It is the **heddle**

> that lifts the thread
> that parts the warp
> that moves the shuttle
> that carries the woof
> that is beaten firmly
>> — **into cloth.**

It is the **loom**

> that women use
> that weaves the linen
> that makes the sails
> that powers the ship
> that carries the refugee
>> — **to freedom.**

1995

Contents

Prologue

The Last Look

As excited as Emile Brouchette had been four years before, when he was given the highest honor and greatest responsibility of childhood, he was even more excited to pass it on to the next boy. Now he could be free to follow his passion. More than anything, he was eager to go out in the fishing boats he had watched for so long from the cupola above the Huguenot church.

There would be perils at sea too, where fishermen were at the hands of God and nature, but that couldn't be more fearsome than the perils on land, at the hands of man.

The post he was handing over to the next young Huguenot boy would safeguard the congregation of the tiny square church that overlooked the harbor of La Rochelle, France.

Strife over how to worship the same God had been at the heart of the escalating conflict in the 1600s between believers in Catholicism and the Calvinists of France called Huguenots.

Emile was up early. He waited for the pastor's knock at the kitchen door. They exchanged whispers as they walked up the hill toward the church. Dawn broke the eastern skyline to silhouette the simple, square Huguenot church that had risen against the sky some 60 years before.

As his beloved pastor pulled the heavy wooden door open, he said quietly to Emile: "Job well done. You've kept our congregation safe for these four years. Godspeed in whatever you do from now on."

Once inside, the pastor pulled the door closed and secured it firmly. With warmth in his eyes, he watched Emile climb the risky steps and the shaky rope ladder up to the cupola for the last time. The boy squeezed through the small opening, as the designated look-out to assure security for the congregation of their surrounding community.

Part I

Charles' Story

The square Huguenot Church and its octagonal cupola is surrounded by a graveyard of brave believers.

Chapter 1

Sounds of Peril ... Sounds of Joy

The sound they heard was faint but certain. Everyone knew. Everyone gathered.

Seven-year-old Charles Germaine and his sister Madelaine, two years younger, led the family up the hill to the Huguenot church. An elderly Frenchman, stooped from hauling fishing nets all his life, stood outside the heavy wooden church door. The children knew only too well why he was there and why the door was now hinged to open out.

Earlier arrivals sat facing them as they walked down the center aisle to the third pew on the right. The rest of the family quickly followed, filling the pew. Charles and Madelaine, being the oldest children, were charged with keeping the two-year-old twins under control.

At the end of the first prayer, Charles opened his eyes to see one twin disappearing beneath him. Madelaine was quick to retrieve the other who was making a noisy getaway under the pew just ahead.

That pew was occupied by their grandparents, as it had been for many decades. It was the well-deserved seat of honor in front of the pulpit which held the bible. The church bible was significant and revered not only for the scriptures, but because it was the place of record of births, baptisms, confirmations, marriages, and deaths in the congregation.

Grandfather Germaine was a young boy when he helped his father to build their church, the first Huguenot church, in the fishing village of La Rochelle, France. Now there were five more in this successful, fast growing community. La Rochelle was

Walloon Provinces of the
Belgic Lands
in the 17 Provinces of
The Netherlands in the 1500s:
Hainaut, Namur, Liege, and Luxembourg

homeport to ships built by local Huguenots in the mid-1600s.

Charles had heard Grandfather Germaine relate how in his youth he had helped his father, a cordwinder, make the rope for the ladder that was essential in their lives and their spiritual well-being. In the eyes of his family, the status of the rope ladder ranked just below the pastor's pulpit.

As first-born, Charles was automatically charged with handing down their family history and church beliefs to the next generation. He listened to pertinent details from the pulpit and from family discussion around the supper table. Some of these he could grasp now; others he would understand better as an adult.

Charles knew that for more than a century Huguenots had been devoted followers of French-speaking John Calvin. Every child learned how Calvin had presented his ideas of reform in

Switzerland less than 20 years after Martin Luther, the German priest, had advocated drastic changes in the Catholic church.

Calvin's ideas had also spread to the French-speaking Walloon Provinces of the Belgic lowlands north of France. They were part of the 17 Provinces of The Netherlands, all of which was under the control of Spain and the Holy Roman Empire. The original intent of these Walloons in the mid-1500s had been to bring change within the Catholic church, not abandon it.

Although the Catholics and these reformists continued to worship the same God, the Calvinist reformists wanted to pray to Him directly, not through the saints, as was customary in Catholicism. Each side became more convinced their beliefs were right.

At the risk of their own lives, the French Huguenots crossed the border to help these Walloons. Through their combined efforts about half of the Belgic Walloon population became Calvinist followers. They called themselves Walloon Reformists, not Belgic Huguenots, as they are often referred to erroneously.

Early hot-beds of faith formed along the River Scheldt in the adjacent Hainaut Province. The reformed movement was rife throughout the four Walloon Provinces that later became known as the Spanish Netherlands.

Disappointed by lack of any response to their demands for change within the church by their priests, or by the Pope, the Walloon Reformists decided to take matters into their own hands. What happened next threw everyone into turmoil and threatened the supremacy of the Catholic church.

Charles listened to his grandfather and his father as they sat across from him at the supper table. His grandfather explained what had happened: "One night in August 1566, Walloon Reformists entered more than 400 Catholic churches, monasteries, and convents throughout these provinces." He shook his head in disbelief at the barbaric actions of those Calvinists, while at the same time recognizing how extremely frustrated they had become.

"They smashed the statues of all the saints and they lopped

off the head of the Virgin Mary, at each site." Charles was taken aback when he heard this, although he had never seen a church statue, nor did he have a clue about the deep sanctity Catholics felt about the Virgin Mary.

His father added, "You can bet that set off a fire storm! In fact, it started a revolt in 1567 that lasted two years. The Catholics began to call the revolters 'protestors' and the name Protestant has survived."

"The Walloon Reformists fled for their lives, going north to Holland and east across the German border. Hundreds of them migrated south throughout France," his grandfather continued. "Charles, some of the Walloons who came to La Rochelle, are your own ancestors."

At only seven, he couldn't understand all this history, let alone the geography, but he knew he would be responsible for passing it on. He was overwhelmed and confused. He wanted answers. "Grandpa, that was a hundred years ago. Why are the Catholics still mad at us?"

Together his father and grandfather tried to explain to him, "Priests feel that when people become Protestants, it takes away their own power and the influence of the Catholic church over people's lives."

"Now they want to snuff out the lives of those who don't agree with them. And I can see why they are angry. They know that none of the money earned by successful Protestants will ever support the Church of Rome."

His father looked across the table. "Does that make it clearer for you?"

Charles nodded in silence. It was still hard to comprehend. What was easier to understand, was the fear and apprehension of those all around him.

What astonished him most was to hear that some Catholic priests urged their parishioners to carry out personal assaults on Huguenots. Additionally, the Catholics targeted the Huguenot's businesses and even their houses of worship. Charles and Madelaine already knew about locally organized groups, the dreaded "dragonnades," and what they could do.

Like other Huguenot churches, this was a simple, square building aimed at avoiding easy identification. Constructed of thick stone and coated with masonry of the time, the walls stood 15 feet high. A single door was installed on the north side, as was the Huguenot custom.

Outside this door and around the building were thin grave-stones. It was also Huguenot custom to bury people with their heads to the north. Some of the stones, already tilting with age, signified the graves of older generations. Many had given their lives for their firm Calvinist beliefs.

Opposite the door were the only windows; they faced south. These had been their escape route a few years before. Attackers hid nearby in the graveyard early one evening. As late-comers arrived for service the dragonnades burst through. This had occurred only a week before Charles was born, but he had heard these details so often, he almost felt he had witnessed it himself.

In addition to the boy in the cupola, a guard on the ground watched for anyone lurking under the eaves that the boy was unable to see. Together they would determine when it was safe for worshippers inside to leave. They reinforced the door for safety by attaching a long, heavy piece of wood to slide across the door-jamb. That defied even the strongest avengers.

There were double sets of wooden blinds at each window. One set opened out, the other opened in, and both could now be bolted shut. With this security, the congregation could concentrate on the service.

In contrast to the gold-ornamented altar of the Catholic churches, simplicity defined this interior. There was no altar, nor any statues. The simple wooden pulpit was unadorned, aside from the two-foot square Huguenot cross attached to the front. As a young man, Grandfather Germaine had carved it of one-inch thick poplar. He showed Charles how he had smoothed the gentle curved edges with a sharp mollusk shell.

Charles and Madelaine had often picked up mollusks as the waves from the Atlantic Ocean pounded the shore. They tried to

The pulpit, Huguenot cross and Bible

see who could find the largest one, or the rare one that was closed, with the mollusk still inside. These shells were about three-inches long, with a dark, flaky surface on the outside. The two sides were usually gaping open, and near the center hinge the shiny inner surface was purple, tapering to snow-white at the rim.

Their grandfather demonstrated how he had polished the surface of this large cross by first scattering sea salt and wet sand over it and then pushing a block of wood back and forth until it was smooth.

They also knew it was the tradition at their church, for him to carve a similar cross three-inches in size for each child as they reached adolescence and were confirmed. That was the moment they vowed to follow the Calvinist faith in devotion and humility. In the coming years it would be confirmation time for Charles, then Madelaine, and the long row of siblings to follow.

Charles and his family listened to the scriptures the pastor read by candlelight. Even in daylight, Huguenot churches were so dimly lit, candles were needed at the pulpit.

Not wanting to be noticed by the Catholics, the Huguenots avoided a steeple or the sound of church bells to call people to worship. Instead they devised a clever alternative. A young boy was chosen to carry a conch shell that was six-inches to eight-inches long and climb through a small opening to the unobtrusive cupola above. This conch shell was unique because it had been ground against a rock to flatten one end. The sound from this conch shell helped coalesce and protect the lives of those Huguenots within hearing distance.

As another church was built, a similar conch shell was given to the next congregation, maintaining cohesion and continuity within the larger Huguenot community. It was the blunt-ended conch shell that was crucial to their survival as individuals, as a congregation, and as believers to perpetuate their faith.

When the boy in the cupola blew into the flattened end of the shell, a softly-cushioned sound resonated only as far as the safe perimeter of the small community the church served. As a further safety measure against the dangers that beset them, services were called at random times. So it was today for Charles, Madelaine, and all the Germaines.

Blowing the conch shell from the cupola was not only an exalted position within the community, but a very risky one as well. After tucking the conch shell safely in his clothing, the boy first had to climb the steep, narrow 15-foot high staircase, located just inside the door.

Not only was there no protective railing, at the top he then had to make the treacherous transfer to the hemp ladder that was suspended beneath the sloping ceiling. It would take skill and daring. This young boy not only had to clutch the unstable sides with his hands, but he had to cling to the flexible rungs of the ladder in his socks.

At the top he would gently edge the trap door open with his

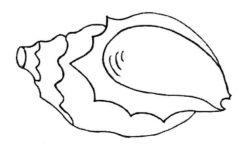

A large conch shell, with the end ground off, was used as a call to worship, or to sound an alarm.

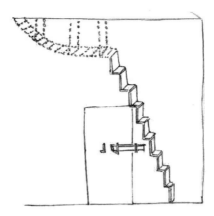

The treacherous staircase and rope ladder led to the cupola above.

head to see through the opening. Before he climbed into the cupola, he made certain there were no draggonades lurking in the churchyard or adjacent streets. Only then could he act on the pastor's instruction and call people to service. He had to remain on look-out during the service and ensure their safe exit before they headed home.

Coded sounds from the conch shell informed the neighborhood what actions they should take. After the boy filled his lungs with crisp, fresh air from the sea, he would blow hard into the conch shell opening. Deep tonal sounds resonated from the curved chambers and bonded all who shared its cherished meaning.

The call to service was a soft, heavenly tone repeated in sets of five sounds at a leisurely pace. The sounds they dreaded, were the three rapid blasts. He would wait a few moments before repeating the alarm. If the congregation needed to gather at the church for safety, the two codes were repeated, one after the other.

That summer day in 1668 the church service would be special on two counts. First, the youngest Germaine sibling was to be baptized. The baby was dressed in a long, white linen dress. It had been used over the generations, and at the earlier baptisms of all the dark-haired youngsters who were sitting in this pew beside their parents.

The cloth for his garment was hand-woven with care. It had originated from the brownish, natural-shaded, course strands of flax. Following decades of gentle laundering, it had become soft and pliable white linen. This garment would be worn by more babies from this pew that would be baptized in the years to come.

This day was also special for another reason. It was the day the pastor was scheduled to announce who would replace the 12-year-old Emile, who was getting too big to crawl through the opening. In this close-knit community of 20 or more families, it was a day of great excitement. Three generations of the Germaine family watched and waited.

Everyone wondered, some even speculated, about whom among the young boys of this tiny community would be so honored. The name would be announced. Faces across the congregation would smile at the boy and his proud family.

A boy who sat across the aisle from the Germaines, stood when the pastor called his name. He moved forward, toward the narrow stairs built against the north wall. The admiring congregation, the boy's family, and the pastor all watched as he climbed the stairs ever so slowly. He grasped the shaky hemp ladder that Madelaine's Grandfather Germaine had helped to make as a young apprentice cordwinder.

In silence, they waited. And they waited. Something unexpected, unpredictable, even mysterious happened. The boy came to a halt as he grasped the rough hemp. Minutes passed, until the boy's father had to go up the risky stairs himself, to rescue his son. No one could rescue him from the humiliation.

The pastor broke the awkward silence. Turning toward this congregation he said, "Charles Germaine, please come forward." Charles could hardly believe his ears.

Now he, Charles, would be the one who would call people to service, alert them at the sign of danger, and be fully honored by the congregation. His sleek, agile body would fit through this constricted opening for another three or four years.

This honor came with a price through no fault of his own; it would haunt him in years to come.

Chapter 2

Off to Sea

"One…"

"Two…"

"Three!!!"

Charles Germaine counted out the numbers in slow cadence during the long minutes it took for the tip of each mast to pierce the morning fog. Barely aware of how soaked his pants were from sitting on the wet grass, this 24-year-old man stood and stared in a moment of awe.

"Here at last!" echoed in his brain. No one in town could be more excited than he as the harbor fog lifted.

"It's *her*! She's *here*! It's *L'Esprit!*" Over and over, Charles shouted as he ran from the distant hillside above the Huguenot church and the Atlantic coast fishing town that cupped the harbor at La Rochelle.

On a clear day, he could have seen a tall steeple and glittering gold cross in the small Catholic enclave far to the south. While nourishing their souls, their lives stayed ill-nourished and impoverished by the demands to support this costly building, its priest, and the Pope.

The whole town had been waiting for this caravel to return to homeport. Now it would be only a few more hours to wait for high tide so the Captain could bring it in to the dock. Then *L'Esprit* would be greeted by the high spirits of everyone. Weeks before, Charles had been selected by the Huguenot owner of *L'Esprit*, to sign on as sailmaker for the next voyage. He would be among the first to board her, to greet his future Captain, and meet the crew.

This Huguenot had grown into a tall, burly young man with broad shoulders. He had become hardened by making sails and hoisting rolls of them onto ships at dock. He had followed in the footsteps of his father and Grandfather Germaine before him, along the waterfront at La Rochelle.

As a life-long cordwinder, Grandfather Germaine had, in his youth, made the flexible lines that held the sails. In his more experienced years, he carefully wound multiple strands of cordage into the heavy rope that secured sailing vessels to the iron chocks at dock.

As age caught up with him, he changed his endeavors to a less rigorous, sitting job, joining his son sewing sails. That was easier on his aching knees and his bent, gnarled knuckles.

Young Charles found life on the waterfront was too tame. He wanted more excitement, more adventure. Adventure was in their blood. After all, it was from La Rochelle that Samuel de Champlain sailed for the New World in 1609 and discovered the lake that carries his name.

Stories Charles heard on the dock still promised plenty of adventure, but it was more than adventure that was driving him. As a devoted Calvinist, and Huguenot, he knew how much he needed to pursue this drive to preserve his faith.

Far back in the memories of most Frenchmen was the 1598 Edict of Nantes. It proclaimed that Protestants throughout France had the right to worship freely. By the time Charles was born, matters had deteriorated greatly. The Catholics wanted to outlaw the Protestants. By the time Charles was an adult, the conflict had reached an even more perilous level.

In 1685, King Louis XIV officially revoked the Edict of Nantes, thus robbing Protestants of this rightful protection. It put all Huguenots at risk. Many were forcibly exiled. Others sought refuge in Germany, The Netherlands, England, and America.

Ships known to be owned by Huguenots had become increasingly vulnerable, especially those whose homeport was La Rochelle, a hotbed of protest in the mid-1600s.

Ship owners and their Captains searched for sturdy crewmen. The owner of the caravel *L'Esprit* hired Charles as much to help protect the ship, as for his skill as sailmaker.

Charles was familiar with the sails required for caravels such as this, still in use in the 1600s. This particular caravel conformed to the unique characteristics of that type of sailing ship: it had the traditional wide bow, high narrow poop deck above the bulging cargo hold, and three square sails. Charles knew these were much easier to make, and mend, than the triangular lateens sails that interspersed the square ones on some of the caravels.

Caravels mainly carried cargo, although they could accommodate 100 passengers instead. On their usual route from La Rochelle to London, and then on to Bordeaux and back, the principal cargo was hemp and sails from La Rochelle, rum and molasses from London, and wines from Bordeaux.

Today, Charles watched as the anchor was dropped. Lines were cast toward the dock, caught and cleated to the chocks to keep the ship safely moored at the wharf in high tide or low.

The Captain of *L'Esprit* stood on deck to watch as the gangplank was lowered. Everyone on the dock cheered and Charles ran up the gangplank to reach the deck first.

"Welcome aboard." The Captain greeted him with a hearty, familiar voice.

"Thank you, Captain. I've been assigned to your ship as sailmaker." Charles tried to keep his exuberance under control and appear suitably seasoned for the task.

"You'll be a great sailmaker for *L'Esprit* with all your experience. I've watched you over the years, trained as you were through your father's skills as a sailmaker and your grandfather's years as a cordwinder for the rigging."

Charles shifted his weight to the other foot, somewhat embarrassed by the Captain's praise.

"Why, I was there the day you were named to blow the conch. I was sitting in the pew right behind you and your sister and the curious little twins."

Charles chuckled at the memory of the adventuresome pair, now in their late teens.

"You couldn't have been more than six or seven. I remember it well when your name was called."

"That was some surprise!" Charles dropped his voice as he said, "I was both sad and glad."

"But you served well, just as I expect you will on *L'Esprit*." The Captain tilted his head to the left, and rubbed his graying beard, taking a long, studied look at this newest member of his crew. Then his broad, calloused hand landed firmly on Charles' shoulder giving him a feeling of reassurance not even words could convey.

"Aye, aye, sir." Charles' reply marked his own high spirits.

Hopefully, the Captain would recognize that along with his heavy-set stature, Charles still seemed to have an easy-going personality. Since the two of them would be sharing the forward cabin, this trait was as important as his knowledge of how to make the ship's sails. Tight as these quarters were, Charles knew the top bunk was preferable to the crowded, stuffy quarters below deck where the crew slept in hammocks of scratchy hemp.

The caravel *L'Esprit* was headed for England, as it would be for another three or four more trips before spring. During these trips the Captain would have plenty of time to determine whether Charles had the personal qualifications as well as the technical skills, of equal importance for the rigors of a long ocean voyage.

Measuring, cutting, stitching, mending, and rigging the sails fell to the sailmaker, or to crewmen under his supervision. From the mizzen mast to the main sail, tears often had to be mended during full sail. Sometimes this meant climbing the rigging in storm-tossed winds. Helping Charles to rig the sails, and especially to tie proper knots, would fall to another novice seaman from La Rochelle.

To make the sailmakers job easier, the women who wove flax into sailcloth set their looms to place two adjacent blue threads in the warp an inch from each edge of the 20-inch wide yardage. These lines were used to guide the sailmaker's three-inch-long triangular, blunt-edged bone needle in a straight line to part the threads, not cut them. Another line sewn along the selvage edge on each side preserved their full strength.

A week after it had docked, *L'Esprit* was preparing to leave. Charles bid farewell to his parents and his many young siblings who still lived at home. Madelaine, his favorite sister, had married the boy next door and moved to St. Felix a few years before. Charles had traveled there only once, a two-day journey on foot. He helped them build their little cottage beside the flax fields where Pierre had gone to work for the Lord of the Manor.

Waving goodbye to his family, Charles swung a heavy canvas sack over his shoulder. With a bounce in his step, he whistled as he kept a brisk pace along the dusty street to the wharf.

As Charles neared the dock where *L'Esprit* was moored, he could hear the waves lapping against the hull. He gazed up at the tall, slender masts with reverence and respect as they swayed slowly back and forth. He was eager to help the sailors unfurl the sails and prepare to leave at high tide. This would be his new home, his hope for great adventure, and a new future.

One evening Charles and the Captain sat on the lower bunk, conversing comfortably, more as hometowners than two men as widely separated by rank as they were.

The Captain reminisced. "That was quite the honor when you were chosen, and you were only seven you say?"

Charles replied: "It wasn't my honor, sir. It came to me by default."

"Not at all, you were right for the task, and its honor. You performed it well, my lad."

"But, don't you see, someone else had to fail, for me to have the chance."

"It wasn't any easier for you, to climb up there, Charles. You met your obligations for nearly four years, didn't you?"

"That's not enough." He paused quite a while. "I've always

felt that failure would catch up to me, too." His head sagged as he fingered his seaman's cap a few minutes until he confessed, "I used to dream about that as a child."

"Well, that's all behind you now. It will be *bon voyage* from here on."

That night, less than a week out of port, the seas were stormy. The bunk rocked and creaked. Charles slept fitfully, tossing and turning between catnaps.

Then, shortly before he was shaken awake to go on watch, it happened:

It was the first time since he was an adolescent that the dream—no, the nightmare—was so vivid.

Once awake, he shook himself, to establish that he wasn't really trapped in the cupola like a bird in a cage. Moments before, the nightmare confirmed his fear of failure for what seemed an eternity. There he was, unable to get down through the trap door. He was wedged fast, growing larger and larger, his shoulders too big to squeeze through, trapped for life! *Help! Help! Help!* He shouted at the top of his lungs from the cupola. But that was the last thing anyone on watch for dragonnades would expect to do.

Now that he was awake, he worried that the Captain had heard his cries for help.

Had he actually cried out? Had he lost his chance to be on the next Atlantic voyage that was highly rumored on board? Had he ruined any chance to fulfill his dream? Had he truly failed?

Chapter 3
L'Esprit's Earlier Voyage

Several years before, the Captain of *L'Esprit* had sailed to America on the same caravel. It had arrived in the beautiful, broad harbor at the mouth of the Hudson River. The ship docked at Manhattan Island's newly built municipal wharf near Water Street. This was the ship's destination for the highly prized cargo of red Bordeaux wine, along with rolls of hemp rope from La Rochelle.

Charles had heard rumors from his shipmates that the Captain was planning another trip, but that was yet to be confirmed. Every time the rumor surfaced, he could feel his heart beat faster.

He was curious over what the crew could tell him about their experiences in America. Four of the older, more experienced mates had been on *L'Esprit's* remarkable voyage. They relished the opportunity to tell their sea yarns to this novice, who then had to separate fact from fiction the best way he could.

Charles had to re-construct for himself the probable sequence of these snatches of history. For certain, he knew that in 1609 Henry Hudson had discovered the river that now bore his name, as he was in search of the highly sought westward route to China for the Dutch.

Neither Charles, nor any one else on board could have known, what a failure Hudson considered himself to be. He was all the more distraught, because he had already tried and failed on two previous explorations to find a polar route to the Orient.

Sitting around after the evening meal, in the light of an oil lantern, Charles caught the briefest glimpse of one bearded seaman, as he winked at another across the table. He was beginning to realize when he was in for another well-embellished yarn. Others chimed in, with further spin. Their excited voices revealed the entertainment they enjoyed whenever a new seaman joined the crew.

The next evening a white-bearded shipmate sat down beside him and began to tell him a story, one that would surely have seemed to be spin, had it not been for his tone of voice. Also, Charles had had clear discussions with him on prior occasions, about the settlement at the tip of Manhattan Island. Even so, Charles was wary as he listened. What he heard seemed unbelievable.

The seaman started by saying, "The Dutch returned to this newly discovered river as traders. They bought tobacco and beaver pelts from the Indians, but they always returned to homes in Amsterdam and to sell these wares at a handsome profit."

He looked Charles straight in the eye, "It was really the Walloons who were the first settlers."

Charles jumped off the bench. He steadied his sea legs as well as he could in the storm-tossed ship and tried to steady his mind with this unexpected piece of information. Immediately, in his mind, he became a youngster back at the family supper table, hearing his father and Grandfather Germaine tell him about the Walloons.

"You can't mean it! So, you say, it was not the Dutch, but the Walloons, who first settled the Dutch territory!"

"That's right! I'm telling you, it was the Walloons who arrived with families, flax seed, and farming tools. They came to stay."

"So when was this?"

"They arrived from Amsterdam on a ship named the *Nieuw Nederlandt*. The year, they say, was 1624, but I hear it could have been a year earlier." The old seaman drew hard on the long-stemmed clay pipe, a proud purchase of his trip.

Charles sat down hard on the narrow bench that was firmly secured to the deck. His mind was far away. In silence, his thoughts were tugged back to La Rochelle.

As a child he had heard Grandfather Germaine tell about the hundreds and hundreds of Walloons who like the Huguenots, were close followers of John Calvin. Many who had come to La Rochelle from the Belgic Lands were among his own ancestors.

He remembered hearing how they had fled the Hainaut Province just north of the French border in the mid-1500s. They were tortured for being protestors against the forms of worship they objected to in Catholicism.

The Captain joined them for his supper. Soon he confirmed what the white-bearded man had just told him. "My family used to tell stories of how the Walloons had fled to France along the River Scheldt during the two-year revolt." Then he went on to describe how, in 1567, the Duke of Alva had been sent from Spain to stamp out these audacious revolters by revenge and torture.

"They had to flee because they were Calvinists, you know. And, now it is the Huguenots that the Catholic church is determined to eradicate." The captain sighed. "Most of my ancestors in La Rochelle were Walloons. Now that we are being persecuted as Huguenots, it would seem like double jeopardy."

Charles watched him lower his head as if to reflect on what had sadly befallen them, over so many generations.

"So if I can ever get to America, you mean to say I may meet people who could be related through my distant Walloon ancestors?" Charles said this as much to himself as the others. Then, he leaned back against the bulkhead, as if it would take time for him to absorb all this history. "So what happened? The Dutch claimed it. Why isn't it still in Dutch hands?"

"That's a long story, but basically, a British Colonel by the name of Richard Nicolls captured New Amsterdam at the tip of Manhattan Island in 1664, without firing a shot."

"Then, a decade later, actually in 1673, the Dutch came back to claim it for themselves. But that was for just a short time… only 15 months in all." A gray-haired crew member went on to tell that the Treaty of Westminster was signed between the

Dutch and the British in June of 1674. It gave the British control of the colony once more. They arrived in November of that year to make good on their claim.

These details mattered little to Charles. What was relevant to him was more personal. He had heard that English was now becoming the prevailing language in the colony the British had renamed New York. He considered what an opportunity he would have to learn this new language, while *L'Esprit* was docked in London.

Chapter 4

Life Aboard *L'Esprit*

There was another novice besides Charles aboard *L'Esprit*. Only the Captain knew his real name. Because he seemed so timid the crew named him Tim. He rarely spoke and had a noticeable stammer. When he faced the Captain, or first mate, it was even more apparent.

As novice seafarers, Charles and Tim bonded in a special way that neither of them could do with the others. Each met the usual harassment of the seasoned crew, but Charles felt Tim got the more blatant, demeaning aspects of learning the ropes. More often it was Tim who drew night watch, followed by cleaning the head, and scrubbing the deck at daybreak.

Whenever Tim was involved in some physical altercation, Charles would try to come to the defense of this slightly built 17-year-old, seven years his junior. Often he would try to meet Tim later to help him cope.

This young seaman came from the far end of town, in the small enclave of La Rochelle's impoverished Catholics. He had been brought up by his grandfather who had spent years at sea. By the time Tim was six his grandfather had taught him a dozen knots used on shipboard, so he really did know his knots. Although it was rare to have a Catholic on board, Tim's skills had been brought to the attention of the ship's owner and he had been hired.

Tim learned the ropes at sea quickly. Charles often watched him climb the rigging like a jungle monkey. Tim could tie or untie the sails with great agility, even when the lines were wet and the salt spray stung his face.

He quickly sensed which topsail knots had to be loosened

first, to keep control of the sail in a strong wind before it was dropped with care to the boom below. Then he would secure it with the designated set of knots. Every knot had its special place to be used on a sailing ship. Each knot was tied in an orderly sequence of movements, but it seemed to Charles that Tim did it with a slightly different twist. Only later did he learn that his grandfather, who had taught him, was left-handed.

Often Tim thought of his grandfather with deep affection and gratitude. Even though Tim couldn't swim his grandfather had urged him to go to sea for the adventure, just as he himself had done. One of the early ships his grandfather had sailed on made a memorable trip to the St. Lawrence River only two or three decades after the notable discovery by their own explorer, Samuel de Champlain. All this interested Charles, but he never wanted to go where the French were in charge of order and religion.

Since Tim had been brought up a Catholic, Charles began to wonder to himself how he might be different. He had never been around a Catholic before. Never in their whole lives would these two young men ever have had the opportunity to know each other in La Rochelle.

The only difference Charles could see—and he really looked—was that in a big storm, Tim would go to his battered old sea bag that had been to sea for 40 years. There, he would pull out his cross and rosary, the same one he had carried when his grandfather had taken him to daily mass. Charles heard the beads clink softly against each other as Tim fingered them. During a storm he muttered his Hail Marys at a more rapid clip.

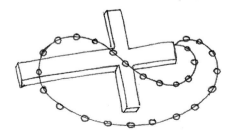

The only difference Tim could see in Charles was that his French had an unmistakable Huguenot accent. Tim had been told that their French sounded different because they had been influenced by the dialect spoken by the Walloons who had migrated there from north of the border. Tim would not have heard who the Walloons were, nor why they had come. He knew only that no one in his part of town spoke with a lilt at the end of a phrase, or used those idioms of expression. Tim and Charles found their differences fascinating more than distancing. Soon their friendship deepened since they faced none of the barriers on shipboard that had been imposed in their own neighborhoods.

Sometimes they would sit quietly for a long conversation. Then Tim's stuttering hardly surfaced. Most of all was the fond warmth each had for his own grandfather that they shared most in common.

Tim hoped to be on the next voyage to America as much as Charles did. They talked about it often. Rumors escalated. It was often the topic at meals when the crew told more and more tales. One tale was about five Huguenots from Bordeaux who had earned their passage to America by loading the cargo of red wine. In the heat of the day these burly men stripped to the waist; black curly hair covered their chests and shoulders. In exchange for loading and unloading cargo they were allowed to sleep in the constricted space between the top of the wine kegs and the deck above. Stormy seas made for a long, rough trip.

The Captain smiled to himself as the crew related their stories. He knew they were, in their own way, trying to pry out of him whether the rumors were true. He was determined that he would reveal his decision at the time and place of his choosing, not theirs. Both sides enjoyed the game. As an outside observer, Charles relished this daily parrying.

One of the crew who had also been on that trip offered, "Why, mate, in the marketplace, you could hear languages from every port. Someone told me as many as 18 were spoken there."

But this was countered by another seaman, also from that voyage who soon chimed in to advise the novices. "The British had been back a few years when we were there two years ago. That was in '83. You can bet if you needed directions, you'd find all the street signs were in English. Learning that language is a priority if you expect to go to America."

By the time *L'Esprit* docked in London, it was a hot and humid August day. It would be a long time to wait for a spring trip to America but the prospects excited Charles. If he met all the requirements to the Captain's satisfaction and didn't awaken him with his nightmares, he too might be on that next voyage. His driving desire was to live, to love, and to worship—in freedom.

Happy that the Captain and he had gotten on well together, he felt reasonably assured the bunk would be reserved for him on the long ocean voyage. Thus he had tried to learn as many English words as he could in London. Back on board however, he found that few of the words the willing English seamen taught him could have been used at his mother's table if they had been translated into French.

He decided that when he got to England next time, he would seek out a nice girl to learn language that would be more appropriate to use in America. This had risks as well. One of the old sailors took Charles aside. "You have to be careful. There are lots of girls in London who can teach you English. The problem is, they have so much to teach you, you could miss cast-off at high tide. It's happened to many a sailor, and they haven't all been new to the sea as you are, mate." Charles smiled, and remembered this sage advice.

When *L'Esprit* cast off from the dock on the Thames it carried a load of rum and molasses that the British ships had brought from the West Indies. The ship's schedule had been altered to now include not two ports of call before returning to La Rochelle, but three. According to nautical superstitions, three ports of call meant very bad luck.

The newly added stop was the small ocean-side Place de

la Coubre, near La Tremblade. They would off-load a sizable portion of the cargo there, before proceeding south along the Gironde estuary to Bordeaux. The Captain agreed to this because the hold would be nearly empty then and they could pick up a full cargo of those fine Bordeaux wines that were cherished by English noblemen and royalty.

Charles heard one seaman complain loudly. "Three ports of call! London...Place de la Coubre, then Bordeaux, before home port. Bad news. How did the Captain ever agree to this? He never had before."

As a novice seaman, Charles dismissed these ominous forebodings but he was deeply attentive whenever the topic of America came up. With more frequent assaults on homes, businesses, and ships by angry Catholics, it was becoming a matter of growing urgency to flee for one's safety and sound future.

Early in the voyage, Charles had learned of the faith the crew had in knowing there was a caul hanging in the wheelhouse. Legend had it that an intact, dried birth sac, called an amniotic sac, or caul, meant that the infant or animal had traversed the treacherous birth canal safely protected. According to sea lore, a caul would give them added protection through treacherous storms at sea. To some, this meant anyone born in a caul could also be clairvoyant.

Men aboard *L'Esprit* felt even more protected since their Captain had been born in a caul. In addition to Charles' sound upbringing in the Calvinist faith, and with his new faith in the caul, he felt secure. What more could anyone need?

Charles felt that he and the Captain had gotten along well together. What was of greater importance in his role as a sailmaker was how he had gotten along with his shipmates. No matter how experienced he was in making and mending sails on dry land, he had to be sensitive about supervising those who knew far more than he about the rigors of the sea. He always treated their knowledge with utmost respect. Indeed it took a special personality and newly developing interactive skills to assume his leadership as sailmaker. This was an especially delicate situation since not only had the Captain known him from his youth, Charles shared the Captain's cabin. It would be only natural for the other seamen to wonder if the Captain would give him an easier time, or exclusively share some hint of his plans.

It was late in August when *L'Esprit* neared the harbor of Place de la Coubre. Charles noticed the crew voiced their superstitions more frequently. Each of them was also growing more anxious to hear for certain if the Captain was planning another trip to America and whether they would be part of the crew. When the ship arrived in the harbor of Place de la Coubre, it was too late to dock safely. Instead, they dropped anchor out in the harbor.

That done, the Captain ordered the sails be secured for the night and climbed down the ladder. He slid to the far end of the galley bench and sent word out for the crew to gather. Numbering ten in all, everyone but the man on watch crowded in, shoulder to shoulder. The atmosphere was tense. All hands eyed each other. They wondered and they hoped.

The Captain cast a riveting gaze down the line at first one, then the next seaman. They stood motionless, silent, anxious. The lapping of the waves was the only sound. Then he announced, "*L'Esprit* will set sail for America in April."

As much as everyone wanted to shout, they maintained their disciplined silence so as not to jeopardize what he was likely to announce next.

Slowly the Captain called out names of the men who would be on that crew. First were the four crewmen who had been on the previous voyage. To this he added four more, Charles among them. The two remaining sailors would learn whether they had qualified only after the ship docked in La Rochelle. One of those was Tim; the other was the man on watch.

Once the Captain dismissed them, great excitement broke out and one sailor climbed the ladder to tell the man on watch the good news and the bad. Although he was not yet named, he still had a chance.

After the Captain had made his announcement, he set out the details of his plans to re-stock provisions in La Rochelle for *L'Esprit's* trans-Atlantic voyage. Then they would sail to England, and take the final steps to prepare the ship.

Just thinking about being home for more than a week excited Charles. This would give him extra time to be with his family. He knew if he went to America, it was unlikely he would ever see them again.

It was during the late-night watch that tragedy struck. A band of ruffians rowed out in a skiff and climbed aboard. They demanded that Tim, the deck-hand on watch, bring up a hogshead of rum from the cargo hold. If he didn't, they threatened to toss him overboard. Not only was Tim afraid of drowning, he was so frozen in fear he could not even yell an alarm.

Sailors tried to avoid facing the Captain's Mast, the onboard discipline. So would Tim! As soon as he came off watch he hid in the cargo hold. Whereas the Captain was fair-minded and well respected, he could still hand out harsh punishment to anyone whose actions jeopardized the safety of his ship or crew. Tim had heard dire tales of what the Captain could impose on anyone for breaking the rules of the sea. Sadly it would be others on board who would be the first to pay the price for his silence, a silence imposed not by intent but by his life-long speech impediment.

At daybreak the crew watched from deck as the red ball of fire rose slowly over the water. They knew it would be a hot day. The Captain ordered the crew to move the cargo designated for off-loading up on deck before it got any hotter.

After docking, these hogsheads were rolled down the gang-plank. Charles and a few shipmates were stacking the drums of rum in orderly rows on the wharf.

Without warning they suddenly came under attack. A band of dragoons, fortified by the rum they had confiscated the night before, seized Charles and three others they suspected of being Huguenots.

Burly as Charles was, he might have overtaken any one of these bludgeoning brutes, and thrown them into the water. In a three-to-one ratio however, he and the others were helpless to defend themselves against this band of a dozen dragoons. Intoxicated, they were even more vicious; they were out to kill.

Dragoons were a more violent version of the dragonnades who had threatened Huguenots in La Rochelle. They dragged the four crewmen, those who were dead and those still alive, by the heels, throwing them haplessly into a wagon.

Only Charles and another seaman lived through the beatings. Worse than death, they faced life in prison at La Tremblade operated by local Catholics.

There was now no hope of Charles going to America or of seeing his loved ones again. How could he hope for his own survival from harsh prison treatment that was designed against it?

While the ship was still at dock, the rest of the crew gradually pieced together what had happened on the night watch. The Captain was informed and the crew was ordered to search the ship for Tim.

Sheepishly Tim crawled up from below. He saluted as he faced the Captain who himself stood at attention in the bow. He expected severe punishment. It could mean losing any chance to be on the long ocean voyage he so hoped for. What was in store for him was far worse. He felt his knees hit each other when, in a voice that was more stern than Tim had ever heard, the Captain barked: "Leave this ship immediately!"

Alone at the bottom of the gangplank, Tim was soon captured by the dragoons. No one among them could have had any idea that he was a Catholic. His rosary was in his sea bag back on the ship, and despite his best efforts to claim his religious identity, words failed to come. Whatever the Captain would have imposed on shipboard, it paled beside what Tim was about to face imprisoned at La Tremblade.

Part II

Madelaine's Story

Chapter 5

La Rochelle to St. Felix

"Anyone seen Pierre?" Madelaine asked her brother as these two teenagers strolled down the dirt road toward the wharf. He shrugged nonchalantly.

Still puzzled, Madelaine muttered, "Wasn't around yesterday, either."

Nearly five years before, about the time of her confirmation, 12-year-old Madelaine began to notice the boy next door in a very different way. One day she followed him to the shore and with a shy smile, held out her hand. "Here, Pierre, is a shell for you."

Pierre took the closed mollusk, a relatively rare find, and held it carefully in his hand. He smiled shyly and thanked her. This created a new feeling for him on many levels. Most importantly, it signaled her unqualified acceptance of him.

Their bond grew. By the time Madelaine had passed her mid-teens, Pierre knew he wanted her by his side to share his ideas and thoughts. Someday he might even tell her those deeply buried feelings he had about himself. By the time she was 16 their feelings for each other had deepened greatly.

Bordering on desperation, she pleaded silently, "Hasn't anyone seen Pierre?" She hesitated to go next door to inquire, for neither of them wanted their own families to know how serious their friendship had become—not yet.

Days passed. No one could tell her where he was, nor what was going on. To be sure, Madelaine thought, Pierre was different. For some time he had talked about leaving La Rochelle without offering any reason. That was scary. Except for those leaving the country out of fear, no one moved away from their family except to go to sea, and then they expected to return. The fact he even considered moving away made him different from the other boys. That was what she loved. That was also what frightened her. If he left, she would lose a life-long friend and confidant as well as someone she wanted nearby.

He reappeared without explanation. But during this curious absence, she realized she had missed him even more. Yes, she wondered and worried for his safety. After all, these were scary times.

A week or two after his return, his behavior again became noticeably different. Whereas they had often taken long walks together, picking up shells at the shore, now he went alone —or did he? Madelaine was beginning to worry he had found another girl. Could he have found someone he was as strongly attracted to as she was to him? She cried herself to sleep as often now as she had while he was gone.

Madelaine thought strange things were happening all around. Most unlikely was her brother's invitation to come with him one afternoon, to the sail-making shop on the wharf. Never had this happened before. Besides, nice girls weren't to be seen near the wharfs. There at the shop her brother, her father, and her grandfather were all making sails. She watched them unroll, measure, cut, and sew the heavy sailcloth.

Sails made in La Rochelle were not only for the ships owned by local Huguenots. Captains of ships from other ports often bought sails for their caravels when they were in port. The skill of these sailmakers was well respected; their sails were much in demand.

Madelaine was pleased to have such an unusual invitation, and she was attentive to all they showed her. She was especially intrigued to watch her grandfather's aging fingers, still able to sew the sails in his son's shop where he could sit to work.

After a while it seemed to her that there was no further purpose to the visit, so she stood up and headed for the door.

"No! No! Don't leave!" Charles' commanding tone was

different from any she had heard before. That puzzled Madelaine even more, but she stayed until it was time for them to head home.

Three generations of Germaines walked to the end of the wharf and headed up the hill. Behind them they heard shouts: "Wait! Wait!"

Madelaine recognized the voice with mixed emotions. She was ever so glad to hear Pierre's voice coming from the sandy beach, and that he was alone. For a moment, she worried about what he would think of her, a nice girl, being down by the wharfs. She soon dismissed that concern for, after all, she was with three family members.

As they neared their adjacent houses, Pierre and Madelaine lingered behind. Pierre reached out for her hand. A whisper from him, a smile from her hinted at plans to follow.

After the late autumn sun had dipped deep into the Atlantic, Pierre returned for her. To her surprise, Charles came along. Together they walked up the hill toward the Huguenot church. Pierre led her toward the farthest tombstones, while Charles slowly circled the church, on the lookout for dragonnades. It had been years since he had been small enough to look for them from the cupola. He stopped to count the years between 12 and 18 and how that period of time had transpired for him and for Pierre who was almost a year older.

In the quiet of a harvest moon, Pierre took the slender darkhaired 16-year-old in his arms. It was then he revealed the reason for his secretive absence. "I've found work." He lowered his voice to acknowledge the negative side of this news. "It's work in the flax fields at St. Felix."

She gasped, realizing how this explained his absence. In the same instant, she realized the strong possibility he would now be gone forever. Before she could even consider how devastating that would be, she heard him say, "And...and... If you'll marry me, we can move there to live." This time she gasped loud enough that Charles heard it.

It was unheard of for Huguenots not to marry and live

where they grew up, unless they were going to America. That dream would be for later. Other dreams were in their immediate future.

Madelaine thought about it. In less than a minute, Pierre had his answer—an instant hug and a warm kiss.

Pierre came from a long line of La Fountaines who had been hardy shipbuilders, but that work never appealed to him. He wanted nothing to do with attaching the booms or the yardarms to the mast, let alone climbing up to rig the sails. He wanted to stay on the ground.

More than that, he needed to do something that would allow him to prove his worth as an individual. Although he respected the pride of the shipbuilders in their collective achievement, he wanted to so something with his hands that yielded the direct result of his hard work. He reasoned that growing crops would give him just that feeling. Madelaine was struck by the fact that Pierre had always seemed driven to settle outside his hometown. Now he could, since he had found work in the gigantic flax fields of rural St. Felix, working for the Lord of the Manor. He was assured of a plot of ground at the end of the row of cottages where he could build his own. This particular Lord was more liberal than most, indicating that after five years of labor he would be granted ownership to his plot. It was this that appealed most to Pierre, for indeed it would, in the aggregate, be visible proof of what his hands had accomplished.

Sunday service this week would be different. Pierre's family, the La Fountaines, always occupied the pew across the center aisle from the Germaines. Directly ahead of them was the steep staircase to the cupola.

After everyone was seated, Madelaine and Pierre walked through the door together for the first time, careful not to touch hands. All eyes were on them as Madelaine, with Pierre close behind, headed for the front pew. The spot directly in front of the pastor was designated for important announcements such as this.

The pastor opened the service with a prayer. Then he looked

at the shy, young couple and asked them to stand as he announced to the congregation that they had posted their bans of marriage. The wedding would take place a month later. Their families were not surprised. They were pleased. Only later would they learn how this marriage would also mean an unexpected loss for each of them.

Madelaine blushed as they faced each other and Pierre gently slipped a braided flax cord over her head. He carefully adjusted a perfect set of snow-white clam shells at her neck. Then, as was the custom, they turned to face the congregation. What was not the custom in Huguenot churches, was the loud, joyful clapping that broke out as everyone stood. Pierre was astonished. His lips quivered and he struggled to keep control of his emotions—those that could be expected, and those that impacted him even beyond the immediate moment.

Their families and friends all admired the gorgeous pair of pure white pearl-like shells that opened like butterfly wings. Madelaine looked down to admire this delicate symbol of devotion. Only later would she discover how he had carefully carved their initials on the back.

They sat down together for the pastor's sermon but Madelaine scarcely heard a word. Her thoughts were swirling. Gradually she pieced together why Charles had invited her to the sailmaking shop. It gave Pierre ample time to search the beach without fear of her discovery. Then he could find just the right pair of shells, ones as delicate as the pale skin of his true love to inscribe for their eternity.

After they were married, they began the trip to St. Felix, 30 miles to the southeast. It would have been impossible without the loan of her family's donkey and cart, a luxury they would likely never be able to afford. In addition to their meager personal belongings, they loaded the loom her father had made for her. Every Huguenot wife was expected to weave. The simple two-harness floor loom was a customary part of the bride's dowery. Madelaine walked beside the cart during the two-day trip and slept in it at night as it was dry. Her new husband and Charles slept under the cart on the damp ground.

Before Charles returned to La Rochelle with the donkey and cart, he helped them build their cottage. He constructed a half-door for the southern exposure. In the future it would keep babies safe inside while the sunshine poured through the upper half to brighten and warm the interior.

Their cottage, like the others, was about 10-feet by 20-feet with the door centered on the wall opposite their hearth. Openings for a deep casement window each side of the door brought in daylight; wooden shutters inside and out were closed to provide marginal protection from winter winds. The nearby blacksmith taught Pierre how to make the heavy iron hinges and a latch for the door, as well as cooking hooks to mount in the back of the fireplace.

Whitewashed walls reflected the faint glow from the bullrush wick during the long, dark days and winter nights, since they could ill-afford costly candles. Their floor was made of horizontal rows of poplar saplings. Spaces between were filled with clay which became hard and smooth with wear.

As with most working agreements of the time, Pierre was to work the fields every day but the Sabbath. Fees toward ownership of their plot were paid through working the fields to reap an established annual quota of flax bundles. In some families partial payment was supplemented by an established number of lengths of cloth the women wove. They could keep any raw flax and yardage that exceeded the defined amount for their own use or to sell. There were no negotiations. Like the others they accepted their conditions of servitude in a patriarchal society that was slowly divesting its feudal past.

Chapter 6

Madelaine's Dream Fades

Madelaine grew weary as she stood in the low doorway to gaze out on the fields of flax. Tiny blue blossoms on slender reeds flowed in the wind like ocean waves. She tried to steel herself from thinking about the sea breezes that had blown against her face along the shore at La Rochelle. Nevertheless, the memory of the howling winter winds that whistled through the house and the small octagonal steeple above the Huguenot church intruded upon her thoughts.

From her doorway she could see the grand Manor House on the hilltop to the east. This stately home overlooked the fields and the tiny, thatched cottages that lined the northern end of the flax fields. It was distinguished by sets of shutters beside the glazed windows each side of the wide front door. More than anything, this clearly contrasted the difference between the status of the owners who lived on the hill, and the workers who had no windowpanes in their cottages. The lives of these families were sustained by the warm sunlight opened shutters let in during the summer and the heat conserved from the hearth in winter.

The Manor House overlooked the waving fields of blue flax blossoms and the thatched cottages of the workers.

*Madelaine looks out the cottage door to the flax fields beyond,
puzzled by a feeling of deep apprehension that hot August day.*

Madelaine's husband was tilling flax at the far end of the
field. From there the cottages looked like precisely aligned rect-
angles while the mounded outdoor ovens resembled graceful,
sprouting mushrooms. These ovens provided families not only
their daily bread, but a sense of communal strength and warm
shield to fortify them against the harshness of their servitude.

At age 21, this fully matured woman in her third pregnancy
had only a faint memory of the slender frame that marked
her adolescence. What was clear was her memory of Charles

who had towered over her by the time he was seven. Secretly she wished that some of the peace and tranquility from those closely-bonded days of youth might return, if only to give her a brief respite.

Catholic fanatics had made life difficult for the Huguenots throughout France for years, but now that the Edict of Nantes had been revoked, life had become even more precarious. In the fields Pierre had heard that many Huguenots were being forcefully exiled. Some voluntarily fled across the border to the German Palatines west of the Rhine that was more tolerant and even welcomed Protestants. Others sought passage to America. Madelaine and Pierre had dreamed of going there too, but the prospects dimmed further and further with the arrival of each new child.

Sunlight cast a shadow of Madelaine's growing form on the cottage floor that day late in August. A feeling of deep apprehension abruptly flooded over her and then she felt as if her heart had been stabbed, it beat so wildly. Unexplained tears welled up in her eyes. Despite the heat of that summer day, shivers wracked her whole body. Although it was only her third month of pregnancy, it already felt like the fifth. She rested her hands on her hips and automatically thrust her elbows back to balance the weight of her distended abdomen.

Watching anxiously for any sign of her husband, she finally caught a glimpse of him. He was bending low to cut the ripened stalks of flax and tie them into bundles.

She assumed her experience that afternoon was just one more complication of a very unusual pregnancy. Reluctant to cause Pierre further worry about her condition she kept the startling, anxious feelings of the afternoon to herself.

Outside the cottage door Jacques now nearly five, and Jeanne, two years younger, were splashing in the mud with their favorite sticks, excited by the puddles left from last week's rains. Madelaine looked at her little girl with mixed emotions. If only Jeanne hadn't been so headstrong, insisting she drink milk from the gourd like her big brother, Madelaine could have nursed her longer. Then maybe she wouldn't be pregnant again so soon.

Nevertheless, she was grateful her children were happy, healthy, and normally active. They ran first one way and then another on their tiny young legs to explore their surroundings. They circled the big round oven and played with the children of her best friend, Nicole, next door. Nicole and her husband had built their cottage and moved the family there more than a year before Madelaine and Pierre arrived. Her thoughts quickly returned to little Jeanne and Jacques. They still needed her so much. She worried how she could care for them when the new baby arrived and demanded most of her energy and attention. Jacques could feed himself, but he was hardly old enough to help his little sister. When on occasion, he had tried, more food ended up on her face than in her mouth. Much screaming and crying followed. Madelaine reminded herself that things would be better in another year or two when her older children could care for more of their own needs.

That night as Pierre lay down beside her on their lumpy straw mat, he turned to gaze compassionately on his tired wife. Her abdomen seemed like a ball of bread dough, rising more and more each day. The oil-soaked wick of dried cattails flickered beside them. Madelaine's graceful mound was outlined against the flame as she slept.

This mound, the third one they had made together, defined their future more than either of the previous ones. It dashed their dreams of ever going to America. Travel by ship with two young children for a voyage of several months was risky. But it would be out of the question with three. Aside from the stormy seas and scarcity of food, how could they ever manage? It would be impossible for them to carry an infant and help the other little ones, along with hauling their belongings and all the food they would need to survive. Certainly they would have to change their plans. What a disappointment! What could they ever do?

Sometimes in the dead of night when neither of them could sleep, they discussed joining the Catholic church just as Nicole and many other Huguenots had done for personal survival. Madelaine readily rejected this solution. For her, as a child born of Germaine blood, that would be impossible!

It was after one such late-night chat, as Pierre was almost sleep, that she had a sudden flashback. As a little girl, she had often sat on her grandfather's lap to listen to him tell stories while young Charles sat on the floor beside them. He told Madelaine how she was special, having been born in 1664. It was the same year as the 100th anniversary of the death of their reformist leader John Calvin, that had been reverently memorialized at that time.

In retrospect, it seemed to her that this charged her with added responsibility. It would be up to her to uphold these religious beliefs. She could never abandon her beliefs without suffering tremendous guilt. She would be forsaking everything the early Calvinists had stood for, had fought for, had died for, in their protest against Catholicism.

More than that, she would be negating the conscientious work of Grandfather Germaine's father who was among other early leaders in their community who had signed the Peace of La Rochelle on October 28, 1626. This document further confirmed the protection accorded by the 1598 Edict of Nantes, for the Huguenots to freely practice their religious beliefs. How times had changed! How dreadfully disappointed her great-grandfather and Grandfather Germaine would have been.

Persecution of the Huguenots had generally become more severe after the mid-1600s. Members of Pierre's family had been beaten by the draggonades. Friends had been beheaded. Relatives were dragged away from a half-eaten meal to meet their imminent demise.

Chapter 7

Thoughts of Home

Throughout that hot August night Madelaine laid awake worrying about what had happened the afternoon before when her heart pounded and she felt as if she were going to faint. The feeling had passed so perhaps it was a part of being pregnant after all, given that this pregnancy had been so very different. She wasn't superstitious, nor clairvoyant, but she did wonder if something had happened at home. Was everyone all right? Were the draggonades on another killing spree?

The next day she felt unusually tired, unexpected this early when compared to her previous pregnancies. She could weave for only short periods of time. Suddenly, while sitting at the loom, she burst into tears. She leaned back against the cool wall and reflected on all that had happened since she left home.

It had been nearly five years since she and Pierre had been married in their family church in 1680. Madelaine was then a slender bride of 16 years with long dark hair and peach-colored cheeks. The groom was more than two years older, handsome, yet shy in public. Whereas Madelaine had enjoyed the whole ceremony, Pierre was happy when it was over so they could leave for St. Felix.

It had been hard for Madelaine to say good-bye to her siblings, especially Yvonne whom she missed in a very special way. Madelaine had been only 10 years old when she was charged with her little sister's care at the time that their mother delivered her next baby. Of course she missed the twins, Arnet and Annette. The week she was married they had celebrated their 13th birthday. She knew she would miss her mother and her Grandfather Germaine.

Only once did she and Pierre return to La Rochelle. That was for Jacques to be baptized. Since it was a two-to-three day walk, it would have been even more challenging after Jeanne was born, to carry both of them.

Arnet and Annette were so cute and their antics had been such fun to watch when they were little. She had a hard time trying to imagine what they looked like now, at 18. She wondered if Arnet, who preferred to be called Arnie by his friends and siblings, had decided whether to become a sailmaker, shipbuilder, fisherman, or seaman.

Then she wondered if Annette had gotten married already. She could have. How she missed the family events at church—the baptisms, confirmations, and weddings. Sadly, she had not heard of Grandfather Germaine's passing until a year later. Now she feared for the health and safety of all her family.

Whenever she voiced concerns about her family to Pierre she had to force herself to keep from crying. He never mentioned anyone he had left behind and rarely even spoke of La Rochelle. It wasn't that he was unsympathetic to Madelaine but his upbringing paralleled hers principally by the fact that both families attended the same church. Pierre attributed her occasional weeping to the fact of her being pregnant, an event that happened at quite regular intervals. Pierre assumed that after these births she was still in a weakened state and was tearful because she was overburdened. It escaped him how much she really missed her family.

As close a friend as Nicole had become, she was not particularly receptive to hearing Madelaine's feelings and fears for her family back in La Rochelle. Religion had never caused any barrier between them but she wondered whether the fact Nicole had converted to Catholicism made her uncomfortable when she heard Madelaine speak of her own feelings and strong Calvinist beliefs.

Perhaps the current acts of violence by Catholics gave Nicole some feelings of guilt she could not fully formulate in her own mind. But Nicole was the consummate pragmatist. Converting

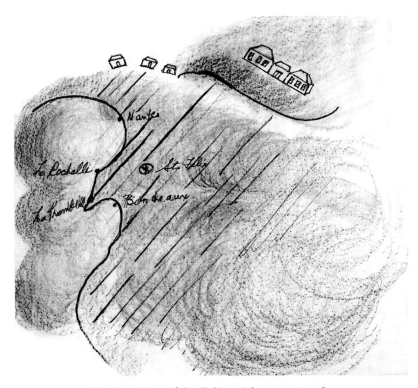

The location of St. Felix with respect to La
Rochelle, La Tremblade, and Bordeaux.

from her original Huguenot roots to Catholicism caused her little personal conflict. Nicole converted simply as a means of coping with the surrounding conflict so that she could preserve security for herself and her family.

Madelaine wondered whether there was another, more compelling reason why Nicole was not as compassionate as she had hoped for. Perhaps Nicole's indifferent response came out of her childhood background. She, like Pierre, had grown up under circumstances that included early family deaths and much hardship. Being homesick was neither part of their experience nor their vocabulary.

Thus Madelaine learned to keep the memories of her siblings, her parents, and her late grandfather to herself, but that was hard. Recalling the endearing sound of the conch shell being blown from the cupola and the hearth-side stories her grandfather used to tell them as little ones helped to create a warm feeling in her heart.

She thought of the sandy beach and all the associations of love it evoked. Automatically she heard the incessant shrieks of seagulls hovering over the fishing boats as they returned with the day's catch.

Most of all she missed having Charles nearby to share her thoughts, her hopes, and their concerns. Focusing her mind on him that day brought a smile to her face. Since they were the oldest, they were closer and had more in common to share with each other than with any of their younger siblings.

She recalled the day Charles had replaced the gangly 12-year-old Emile Brouchette to blow the conch shell, but the memory was enshrined with mixed emotions. Another boy nearly a year older than he had been chosen first. When he was unable to do it, Charles, she remembered, was overjoyed and eagerly assumed this risky challenge.

It brought a broader smile to her wet cheeks to remember the sound of every move whenever Charles had climbed the narrow steep steps, clutched the shaky rope ladder with confidence, and pushed open the trap door. She could almost hear the door rumble and the hinges squeak. After pausing to catch his breath, her brother would balance ever so carefully on the narrow ledge of the cupola to scan the surroundings closely before lifting the conch shell to his lips.

Her thoughts went back further to the feats of their great-grandfather and his brave leadership in La Rochelle. His headstone, like those of other Huguenots, was aligned to the north. For reasons unknown, Huguenots also felt compelled to sleep with their heads in that direction. In America some of their descendants continued this puzzling tradition.

Chapter 8

The Signature

A startling event that had happened the year before, suddenly popped into Madelaine's mind for no reason she could think of. It was so clear, it could have happened yesterday.

She remembered it was a sunny summer morning and she was outside baking bread. She was watching Jeanne, a toddler. Jacques, two years older, was more sure-footed. She was also watching Nicole's children because she and her husband had been summoned to the Manor House.

Madelaine looked up when she saw Nicole bolting down the hill waving a piece of sturdy parchment paper in her hands. Her husband lagged behind. He looked more subdued. When they reached the edge of the flax field he returned to work.

"Look, Madelaine, look at this. We have our paper!"

"What paper? What do you mean?"

"The paper that says the land is ours. Would you believe, the land under our cottage is ours!" Nicole was breathless by the time she reached the mounded oven where the children were playing.

"We've worked for the Lord of the Manor for five years and now it is our land. Just as he owns his land, now we own our land!"

Madelaine had little understanding of this concept. Her family had lived in the same spot for generations. She had never seen land pass from the hands of one person to another, or at least not through a piece of paper. Pierre hadn't really explained to her that someday they too, would own a plot of ground. Even though what was written there had absolutely no meaning for Madelaine, she wanted to show Nicole that

she was impressed, so she held it close and stared at it.

Nicole was barely able to pay attention to her children who were clamoring around her. "And see that line right there?" Nicole pointed to the Lord's handwriting where he signed his name. "We watched while the Lord made these words. It's... his...*signature!*" As she said it, she tucked her chin in and threw her shoulders back to reflect its importance.

"What's a signature?"

"It means he backs up what this paper says. It's his promise. It's proof. That line says my husband has worked for five years. Now he owns the plot. We watched the Lord make his signature. Then he showed my husband the row of marks that were for his name, and he said, 'Now, hold the pen like this and on top of the line make two marks like this. He showed how to make an X on the paper with his finger." Nicole reached down for a twig and said, "Like this," as she scratched the soil in a credible imitation.

Still excited, she pointed to the top of the paper and added, "Look! Those marks all in a row mean our name. Can you believe it?" Then, with a compassionate smile she added, "Madelaine, someday you'll have your piece of paper with Pierre's name on it."

Madelaine couldn't think that far ahead. One day at a time was sometimes overwhelming for her. A few minutes later, she asked, "Nicole, can you write?"

"No, I never had the chance, but I'd like to learn."

Chapter 9

Frightful News

Pierre started home from the fields that day in late October. Madelaine was at the doorway to watch. From far off she could see that he was running. It puzzled her. He was red-faced and out of breath as he approached. What, she wondered, could possibly be the reason.

He held her shoulders and looked into her face for a long moment before he blurted out, "Charles is in prison!" Words caught in his throat. "He was captured and taken to La Tremblade."

Stunned, Madelaine's face turned as white as his was red. He steadied her, fearing she would collapse. They searched each other's face in hopes of grasping some thread of hope. There was none.

She began to shiver, unable to stop all night. Neither the warmth of her husband's arms around her, nor a heavy woolen shawl, nor a freshly kindled fire helped to reduce her chills. Being able to sleep with her head pointed north as Huguenots habitually did, had always comforted her before. This time, nothing helped.

Night and day she pondered what she or Pierre might do. She knew only too well that when Huguenots were captured, they could face torture, or hanging, or life imprisonment by Catholics. Purportedly their crime: worshipping the same God by a different path.

One sleepless night she tried to mentally contact her brother, to send him a message. If only she could let him know that they knew where he was and that they were with him in their prayers, this might help sustain him.

She couldn't go to him and she knew there was no way to send a message since neither she nor Pierre could write. In a flash she remembered how excited Nicole had been last year when she saw the Lord of the Manor write his name and theirs.

Early in the morning Madelaine went next door. "Nicole, remember what you said when you got your paper, that you always wanted to learn to write. I have an idea."

Nicole, who worked regularly at the Manor House, had seen the older children write their lessons for the live-in tutor. As energized as she was over Madelaine's plan, Nicole was cautious as she showed increased interest in their work. She had to be careful not to arouse any curiosity. Nor did she want them to ask questions whose answers they might innocently relay to their parents.

"You don't suppose you could teach me to write, do you?" The children giggled. She smiled, "This can be our secret, one for just the three of us." They giggled again.

It was easy for Nicole to find a quill from a big old turkey in the barnyard. She ground it to a point on a flat rock. Then, she shrewdly devised a way to make ink. In a small amount of water, she boiled the powdery black tips called stamens, that protruded from wild day lilies. She secretly collected stray pieces of paper at the Manor House. She dared not practice there, but she could do so safely at home.

Over the weeks that followed, Madelaine thought about the message for Nicole to prepare. It went something like this:

Dear Charles — We know where you are. We pray for you. Hope you eat. Don't die. We fine. Baby come soon. M.

Madelaine wondered if he would ever get the message. She had to have faith that everyone entrusted with this special piece of paper would pass it along. Worst of all, she feared if it was ever traced back to this source, each of them might suffer.

Chapter 10

Pierre's Paper

Not only was the year 1685 marked by serious national decrees, there were family events, both tragic and treasured. The tragic news of Charles having been captured in August jarred them all. It even overshadowed the treasured event they all had eagerly anticipated in recent months.

Madelaine and Pierre had now been married five years. Five years also signaled to the Lord of the Manor that Pierre's faithful years of service merited him the treasured document. This paper was proof that he had earned rights to own the plot of land on which his cottage stood.

Nicole seemed as excited for Madelaine and Pierre as they were for themselves. They waited for the day of the master's choosing when he would notify Pierre to come. Neither Pierre nor Madelaine had ever been inside the Manor House, so this in itself was an event. Nicole was anxious for Madelaine to see for herself all that she had tried to describe.

Of greater significance to Pierre was that this signed piece of heavy parchment was tangible evidence of his self-worth he could hold in his hands. The intangible pinnacle of this personal milestone was one he alone could appreciate. He stood taller because of it.

As much as Madelaine had looked forward to doing so, she did not even try to join him. It was now December and getting too late in her pregnancy to make the difficult climb. Besides, since this pregnancy seemed different, she was afraid she might deliver early. How embarrassing it would be for it to happen in front of the Lord of the Manor, whom she had never even met.

Often Nicole had told her exciting things about the Manor House. Nicole felt disappointed for no doubt this would be the only time Madelaine would ever have the chance to see it for herself.

"Madelaine," Nicole often exclaimed, "you should see their furniture! The Lady of the Manor told me it even had a name. It is named for our King, Louis XIV. And their windows are amazing. In the front, the glass is so clear, your can look right through them and see the workers down in the field."

Most of all, Madelaine would be disappointed not to watch the Lord of the Manor make those special marks that Nicole called his "signature." She had wanted so badly to see the very moment when his signature magically transfer ownership of the land beneath her feet from the Lord to Pierre. What an event! And all because of the baby she had to miss it.

Chapter 11

Surprise

Madelaine continued as many of her usual chores as she had strength to do. She baked bread every day in the round-domed brick and clay oven that Pierre had built for her the first year they were married. Whenever the wonderful aroma rippled over the air the little ones were close by. They screamed with glee when their mother lifted the round loaves out with a long-handled thin wooden spatula and could hardly wait until it was cool enough to break off a piece.

The days seemed to crawl by. Her favorite pastime, weaving at her loom, was becoming more and more difficult. The loom was Madelaine's pride and joy. She often thought of her father and how she had watched him make it for her dowry. As a good Huguenot wife she wove the long flax fibers into cloth. The heavy scratchy dark gray linen softened with years of washing against the rocks in the stream nearby. That was when it was the best, a lighter hue, soft and pliable. Only cloth that had reached this stage could be used to diaper the babies and not cause a rash.

Babies, babies, babies! Jacques was toilet trained and Jeanne was nearly so. Hopefully she would not need diapers by the time the next baby came but it seemed there was never an end to them.

Today she found that she could no longer raise her leg onto the pedal of this primitive, two-harness loom. She had to use both hands to lift it. Why continue? There was only a short length of thread left on the loom, so it would soon have to be re-warped, for next season's needs. Warping the loom was hard work. It meant she had to lean over, or kneel on the floor, neither of which she could do.

As she sat there, her thoughts drifted back to her home town. More than ever she longed to see her parents, her younger siblings, and the church community she had left behind. It was a luxury she and Pierre had to forego when they moved. As a young bride, deeply in love, she had no idea what a price this would be for her.

Her throat tensed as she reached up to fondle the Huguenot cross hanging from her neck. This three-inch square cross lying against her swollen tender breasts took on the warmth of the milk within.

Her face tensed. A warm tear rolled out of the corner of her eye down the bony border of her nose and into the crease of her mouth. Its salty presence caught her by surprise, drawing her back to the moment of her confirmation at the age of 12. She remembered crying then when her grandfather, who had carved this cherished cross of soft pollard willow, hung it around her neck.

She couldn't allow her thoughts to linger on how much she missed it all—yes, even how homesick she still was. There were more immediate concerns now. How much larger she was going to get? How soon would her baby arrive? It was three or four weeks before she would be due.

That night she had her answer. She awoke and alerted her husband to the pains she knew so well. "Run for Nicole," she gasped between the sharp jabs to her lower abdomen. "And take the children!"

Nicole's husband had originally married her oldest sister who died during the birth of their third son. Then he married their favorite aunt, "Aunt Nicole."

When they first moved here they had built the original cottage like the others, but as their family grew, they had to build on to accommodate the younger ones who followed. It was then that Nicole went to work at the Manor House to help pay for the increased size of their plot.

Nicole and her husband had three children in alternating years. By good fortune more than by plan, she and Nicole had also alternated the times when their children were born. It was only natural for each of them to serve as midwife to the other. Nicole was ahead of her with three births. Now they would be even, or so she thought.

Nicole rushed in. Clean linen cloths hung over her arm. Only last week she had carefully rewashed and folded this oft-used special set of cloths, feeling she should be prepared. She had a woman's intuition that this birth might come early, given Madelaine's extraordinary size. Almost before she could put the cloths down, and get on her knees to help, there was a scream from Madelaine, followed by a cry from the newborn.

"It's a boy." Nicole gently lifted him into a clean cloth. "A sibling to grow up with Jacques. Won't he be happy!" Lusty lungs screamed his presence to all the world in the quiet darkness beside the softly undulating fields of flax.

Nicole cut and tied the cord. She cradled the slippery, wriggling mass while trying to wipe him clean. Holding the tiny body in one hand, she emptied Jeanne's still-warm cradle. Gently laying the baby on fresh linens, she covered him with his father's old jacket.

Jolted at the sound behind her, Nicole turned her attention to Madelaine. A sense of urgency matched grunts of renewed effort. Quickly, another baby emerged, tiny and pink. After hardly a whimper she was content to sleep.

It had been no more than a few minutes since Pierre had left with the older ones. It would be the next morning before they would know how much their world had turned upside down.

Pierre threw open the door, panting from nervousness. Overcome at the suddenness of the baby's arrival, he was doubly shocked to see not only the bundle in her arms, but another in the cradle. Even in the faint light of the burning bullrush wick Madelaine could see his face was white. When Nicole asked him to stir the fire and go out for water, he just looked at her, as if wondering where to find the fireplace. Then she thrust the bundle into his hands, picked up the bucket and walked to the stream to fill it herself.

Pierre hoped that Jeanne would have outgrown her cradle before the arrival of the next child. Now there was no time, she would have to sleep on the straw mat beside her brother on the floor that could be mighty cold in January.

The next day a neighbor came to loan them a small wooden rocking chair with a rush-bottom seat. He had proudly collected cattail rushes from the swamp to make this rush-bottom rocker for his wife to nurse their babies. It had been Pierre's intent to do this too, but Madelaine had delivered this surprise so early, he could hardly think. It seemed to him that life before babies never existed. No longer was it in his memory.

It was a surprise to Madelaine too, although perhaps it shouldn't have been. Twins do run in families, and they surely did in the Germaine family.

When little Jeanne and Jacques came back in the morning, they were curious to see what the fuss was all about. Jeanne looked into her cradle to see two sleeping babies where she should have been.

She cried, waking up both infants. Screams and cries of one baby after another reverberated from the stone and mortar walls of this tiny cottage. Madelaine hardly had enough strength to hold and nurse a newborn without having the three-year-old climbing into her lap for attention, too. Madelaine envied Pierre. He could go out to the quiet fields.

The weary mother often rocked one baby in the cradle with her foot, while she nursed the other. The newborns slept feet to feet. As one kicked the other in the cradle that would soon be too small, they would both be crying, wet, and hungry at the same time. It was a rare occasion when both slept and their mother could take a cat-nap herself.

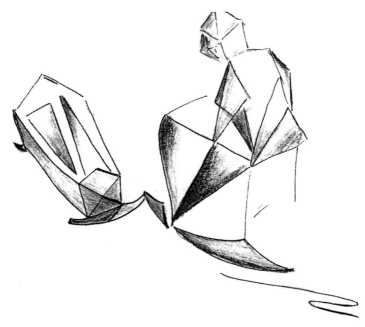

Madelaine rocking her newborn twins

Over recent months she and Pierre had had numerous late-night discussions over the perilous future their children faced. They seriously considered the conflicting prospects. Reluctantly they agreed to relinquish age-old family traditions and their own firm religious beliefs to have the children baptized in the Catholic church.

In the shock of the early unexpected arrival of twins, days passed before they could even contemplate names. They reasoned the names Mary and Joseph would readily convey a Catholic identity.

The twins, now six months old, were rapidly outgrowing their cradle. Joseph was the restless and hungry one. He grew twice as fast as dainty little Mary who rarely cried. He needed a cradle all his own. Borrowing one was the answer, but it made these quarters even more crowded.

Jacques and Jeanne developed their own ways of coping. One

day when Jacques was playing outdoors Madelaine realized she had not heard a sound from him. She got up from nursing the twins, to look for him but he was nowhere to be seen. She called, but to no avail. Jeanne, too young to understand her mother's concern, could offer no help. She was close beside the outdoor oven fully engaged rolling dough for the tiny loaves of bread she wanted her mother to bake.

For minutes, that seemed like hours to the frantic mother, she scanned the fields from the doorway. She finally caught sight of Jacques at the far end of the field in search of his father. After that, he was allowed to trail along, napping in the tall grasses when he got tired.

Little Jeanne tried to accept her uninvited role in life as older sister. One day before lunch the babies were hungry. Both were crying. On occasion she too had been told, "Be a good girl, don't cry." Therefore, good and bad were sufficiently ingrained for her to see the situation for herself.

As lusty cries bounced from the walls she devised her own solution. Bringing in her favorite stick she cried, "Bad baby. Baby cry. Bad baby." Fortunately, Madelaine caught her arm in mid-air before she could bring it down on their heads.

Madelaine had regained enough strength to think about matters beyond their four walls and the fields. She said softly to Nicole: "We must send another letter." Nicole gathered paper at the Manor House and prepared the ink. She wrote this message:

Dear Charles, Twins born. Can't go to America. Must change plans. Flax crop good. Children well. We pray for you. M.

Chapter 12

Fake Converts

They had arrived at their decision after many late-night discussions, disagreements, and with deepened anguish. Now it was time to act. Madelaine tried to hold back her tears as Pierre left. She couldn't.

It was a stifling hot day in August. Pierre might have sought shade, but he was on a mission. He dared not stop or he might turn back. Failure was not an option. He had already had his taste of that.

Pierre heard the measured pace of his feet pound the stone steps of the Catholic church Nicole attended. Without intending to do so, he started to count. At the top he caught his breath! One word escaped: "Four."

He pushed gently on the heavy door, wedging it open a few inches. He wedged it open again and let it shut. The third time, he let himself in. He was grateful to find an empty church. No mass was being said but there was a figure at the altar—his back was turned. Pierre confirmed to himself that he must be the priest. He had never seen one before. He was momentarily struck by the heavily layered robes that were obvious from where he stood at the back of the church. Pierre felt sorry for the priest having to wear so many clothes in this dreadful heat.

He slipped quietly into the last pew and began to look around. Never had he seen anything like it! All that gold, and a lady in blue holding an infant about the age of the twins. Maybe that was Jesus when he was a baby. And who are all those people along the sides? He couldn't see clearly from so far away, so he thought they must be disciples. Then he counted. Something is different here, they've got 14.

Lighted candles, too. Lots of them! He'd only seen their pastor in La Rochelle use a tall single candle to read the scriptures in the darkened sanctuary where the blinds were kept locked for their protection. These candles were smaller and there were many clustered in orderly tiers. Here they didn't need a candle to read in broad daylight. The sun shone through the tall windows. The figures in all their colorful splendor let in plenty of light. To Pierre, it seemed as if patches of color painted the interior in a truly magical way.

Pierre had never been to the other end of town in La Rochelle; it would have been too dangerous. Growing up, the children were cautioned never to go there. Therefore he had never been close enough to a Catholic church to see the windows even from the outside. When he saw them for the first time with radiant sunlight piercing the stained glass, he was in absolute awe. Keeping his silence, he said to himself, "What color, what beauty, what mystery! How could beauty such as this separate people and make them so angry?"

He sat back in the pew to relax. Partly it was because the heat of the day had exhausted him. More than that, he just wanted to absorb it all. The reality of why he was here boldly crept into his consciousness. He wondered to himself, "When did such beauty spawn the determined belligerence that Huguenots face?" Pierre was uninformed about the long-standing history that had perpetuated violence from both sides over the centuries. He had preferred to leave that to Madelaine's side of the aisle.

He sat there quietly, taking it all in. He became so entranced, he was startled when the priest left the altar and started down the aisle. He shivered. What could he say to someone like that, dressed in all the gold threads and finery such as he had never seen nor even heard of?

"And what can I do for you?"

Pierre had never stammered before but he did this time. Finally he was able to compose himself enough to blurt out, "I came...I came to see if you...if you would ba...ba...baptize my children."

"I would be glad to do so," he replied. "How many children do you have?"

Pierre was finally able to say, "Fa...Fa...Four," as he tried to picture how different baptisms would be here. Baptisms at the church in La Rochelle flooded his mind. He felt dizzy. Maybe it was from the heat, maybe not. He tried to re-focus his thoughts. What the priest said next set him back completely. He was stunned at what he heard.

"Unless you are already Catholic, you and your wife will have to convert. Then you can be married in the Catholic church, so the children will be legitimate in the eyes of the Lord." Pierre blanched. He tried to steady himself by grabbing the pew. The brightly colored windows turned black. He could hear the priest saying, "Are you alright?" But his voice seemed far, far away or maybe under water. He tried to reply. He couldn't speak. Then he felt the priest's hand on his shoulder as he said, "Just sit here for a few minutes."

After what seemed to be a long time he looked up and took a deep breath. When he could stand, he thanked the priest and stumbled toward the door. To learn that he and Madelaine would now have to align themselves with believers who had brought violence on his own family and friends was a shock! How could they bring themselves to accept the conditions the priest had stipulated?

To baptize the children, who knew none of this past was one thing. As adults who knew clearly that lives had been sacrificed in the name of the religion he was now asked to adopt as his own, was quite another. It would be even more demanding than Pierre had ever expected. Did this mean he would have to take part in this rampant revenge against others who remained faithful to the Protestant faith? How could he sell his soul this way? He had to, if his children were to grow up and have any lives of their own.

As he walked down the road toward St. Felix his heart was even heavier than it had been earlier. He tried to convince himself that in the steps they would be taking, the children weren't really abrogating the legacy of the Huguenots past and present, but for him to knowingly do so, he would certainly be culpable. That was tantamount to being a traitor, joining the enemy. To face one's conscience and have to fully accept the responsibility for one's own actions, in his mind and in the eyes of God, meant incurring the full burden, yes, the full debt, of guilt.

As he trudged along, he was so deeply engrossed in these troubling thoughts, he scarcely noticed the oppressive humidity of the late afternoon. It seemed that for the first time he could begin to sense how deeply Madelaine experienced her faith. This was in contrast to his family in which practicing religion had been more of a community ritual that helped ensure their collective protection.

The closer he came to St. Felix, the more upset he became. He stopped to sit by the roadside bordered by profuse day lilies and clumps of goldenrod. He needed more time to reconcile the tremendous weight of these decisions before he shared it with his wife. How could he reveal this emotionally shattering news to her? When could he do this with the strength it would take not only to tell her this news, but support her against the forboding demands incurred by a simple request to baptize their children?

When he got home, he simply told Madelaine that the priest had been willing to do so in the next few weeks, but he could not go into any detail yet—for his sake as much as hers. He told her he was too tired to explain more until later. The two-mile trip was as exhausting physically as it had been emotionally.

Still awake in the wee hours of the morning, he reached for his wife. Finally he was able to stumble through the priest's words. She gasped. She had a myriad of questions, but having unburdened himself, Pierre soon fell asleep. So devastating was this news, Pierre forgot to tell her about all the unexpected beauty in the stained glass windows, the colorful statues, and the gold-threaded robe.

Madelaine was far from falling asleep. She lay there pondering, disturbed, and anxious as she tried to absorb the impli-

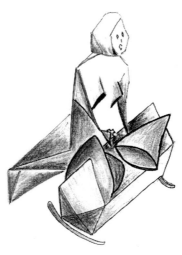

Madelaine burying her Huguenot cross in the babies' cradle.

cation of what she had just learned. She reached for a linen cloth to dry her tears. Then she determined that she would do whatever it would take, to protect her children and themselves.

There were no town records of births, marriages, or deaths. These, plus baptisms and confirmations were kept in the Catholic church. Similar records were kept by the Huguenots. Many of those churches had been looted or burned in the past.

Madelaine sat upright, eyes wide open! Instinctively, her creative mind started to churn. She began to consider how she might use this troubling news as a vehicle to convert a grave disadvantage into a viable advantage. Seizing on the facts that the La Fountaine name would be recognized as being Huguenot, and that the Germaine family had been prominent Protestants for generations, she quickly realized that with no legitimate records, this would be an ideal opportunity to change their identities when they registered in the Catholic records.

Just being able to re-direct her thoughts helped Madelaine deal with the emotional aspect of the priest's demands. As the time drew near to act on the decision that they must make, she would recognize the full impact of what it would mean to her.

Over the next few weeks they debated suitable choices for her maiden name. They finally decided that his would be "Anton," erasing his family name forever. Converted by name as well as by religion at their Catholic marriage, they became Mr. and Mrs. Pierre Anton.

Having joined the church they tried to blend in. Pierre carved a crude wooden cross to hang on the wall to make it less apparent that they were New Catholics, the name given to converted Huguenots. Madelaine sprinkled it with ashes from the hearth to make it look as if it had been hanging there for years.

Initially, Madelaine hid her highly cherished Huguenot cross in the babies' cradle. One Sunday, as Nicole sat down in a pew at the church, she found a Catholic cross. She brought it to Madelaine to wear. As much as she appreciated Nicole's good intentions, it was hard for Madelaine to hold it in her hand, let alone hang it from her neck. In the months to come she forced herself to do so. Outwardly she learned how to sacrifice her own religious practice for the sake of their children. Inwardly, she could begin to rest, knowing her own cross, the one Grandfather Germaine had put around her neck at her confirmation, was safely hidden.

*Madelaine digs a hole to bury her Huguenot cross
at the corner of the flax field near her cottage.*

Chapter 13

Pillaging of La Rochelle

Early in the morning the Manor House cast a long shadow across the flax fields below. As tiny as each blossom was, en masse they formed a faint blue haze. Pushed by the wind, this luxuriant crop of flax moved like gentle ocean waves.

The men were harvesting another abundant crop. Pierre was bending over the knee-high rows of ripened stalks when a friend came up close beside him. In a voice that was soft, but clear, he whispered, "The dragonnades have struck in La Rochelle! Many have been killed…their homes burned."

Pierre's face turned ashen. He thrust his armload of stalks into the man's arms. "Tell the field master I'm sick!"

Numb with shock he walked to the edge of the field. Jacques lay fast asleep in the grass. He called to Nicole's husband, "Bring the boy home when you come."

He walked up the long path to the cottage. Stumbling over a rock, he caught himself before he hit the ground.

What about Madelaine's family, and his own? Were they killed, or were they spared? He wished desperately for a way to find out before he had to tell her.

There was none.

His mind swirled with frightening thoughts. He said to himself, "Tyranny has simply run rampant since the Edict of Nantes was revoked last year."

The goal of these dragonnades was to crush the stubborn Protestants and force them to convert to the "religion of the king." But the Protestants had always been loyal to their king, just not to his religion.

Huguenots had lost their household possessions, their civic

rights, and any "liberty of conscience" as it was called, to practice their own faith. As Madelaine and Pierre knew, between 1683 and 1686, these dragonnades had forced thousands of Huguenots to convert to Catholicism. Persecution may have silenced these rugged Calvinists; it had not altered their beliefs. So it was with this young family.

Madelaine was startled to see him coming home at midday. "Is he sick? Or is there bad news?" Both were true.

She was thin and emaciated. On hearing this news, her face became more drawn. They made immediate plans. Pierre was reluctant to leave her with the four little ones. As he was preparing to leave, a thought flashed through her mind. Maybe he could bring her younger sister Yvonne, now 12, back with him to help her care for the children. Pierre acknowledged through the haze of his anxiety that he would try. He worried about Madelaine and all the little ones while he was gone. Madelaine assured him she would be all right, and that she would ask Nicole to stay with her at night.

For two days and nights Pierre walked through woods, streams, and orchards so as to avoid arousing undue notice. Miles from La Rochelle he began to smell the smoke. Daylight brought sight of the Huguenot community. He gasped. He feared the worst and found it. Ashes were all that remained.

Just below him lay the ruins of their square stone church. Walls alone stood open to the sky, cradling the smouldering destruction for man and God to see. Only the stones in the graveyard preserved any glimpse of this valiant history.

As Pierre neared the remains of the church of his youth, he began to shake. This, the symbol of a vibrant Huguenot community, was devastated. Just as devastating to him personally, was the recollection of his childhood experience there.

He stared. The roof, the cupola, and the pews still sent up faint wisps of smoke. Everything inside may have burned, but the image of the staircase loomed clearly in his mind. Oh, that staircase! The thought of it transformed him instantly. He was no longer the husband who came in the hopes he could bring back help for his over-burdened wife, but the young boy he had once been.

His heart pounded in an accelerated cadence. His breath came in short rapid bursts. Beads of sweat covered his brow, his palms, and his feet.

The memory of that particular day was as clear for him today, as the ocean air had been then. When he heard his name called to blow the conch shell, fear seized him. He felt it in his heart. He felt it in his knees. He climbed the narrow, steep stairs, one dreaded step at a time. He hesitated. Then he grasped the rope ladder. He froze. He could neither go forward, nor could he back down. Long minutes later, with the eyes of the congregation riveted on him, he heard his father's footsteps climb those risky steps. It took the strength of a shipworker's hands to pry his clenched fingers loose.

This traumatic experience had destroyed his self-confidence. It had humiliated him and his family. It had jeopardized his future as a fully respected member of the community. It had contributed to his looking for work elsewhere. It had spawned serious doubts about whether the girl who had shown confidence in him as they were growing up, would even consider marrying him. Would she also agree to move? It had become imperative in his eyes to have a fresh start far from his troubled past. Only then could he regain some measure of self-worth.

Most humiliating at the time was the fact that the next boy in line for this honor was his neighbor who was six months younger. Even more embarrassing, this seven-year-old took to the ropes as if in a former life he had been a seasoned sailor. His name was Charles Germaine.

Emotion and smoke made Pierre's eyes tear. Gradually he was able to get his past fears under control. As traumatic as that childhood experience had been, there was another one he recalled as clearly, the one that had given him his greatest pleasure. It was the day he and Madelaine walked through the door—together for the first time—when their marriage bans were to be announced.

Whereas Madelaine came from a deeply-rooted religious heritage, Pierre's background as a Huguenot was marginal. Having recently converted to Catholicism he had to reassess for himself what it had meant to be a Huguenot and why abandoning his own Protestant ties caused so much pain.

Now more than ever, Pierre could understand how much Madelaine had sacrificed to move away with him when she was so young, when she needed her church, her family and her community to give her support in caring for so many young children. With their recent baptisms, he was acutely aware of how much her family had all had to forego, to have witnessed the baptism of only one of these four little grandchildren.

He reflected on Madelaine's firm belief that everything that happened was God's will. If that was so, how on earth could her God have allowed all this violence and chaos?

Pierre left the church ruins to walk down the dusty street to the spot where their family's homes had been. He found nothing. No one was left of his family nor hers. But behind the ruins of her home he caught sight of the faithful old donkey and donkey cart. He didn't stop, but tried to walk as nonchalantly as he could so as not to be identified with anyone who had lived in La Rochelle. He was fearful for his own life and the safety of his family back in St. Felix.

He walked down toward the wharf. There was little left but smoldering ruins of what had been a thriving shipbuilding industry. He looked past this to the south. On the horizon was a shiny gold cross high above the Catholic church and the neighborhood that surrounded it.

Feelings over having just converted to Catholicism coursed back and forth. One minute he was convinced it was his only means of protecting his family, while the next minute he was overwhelmed by unbound anger against those with whom he had newly aligned himself.

To look at such total destruction of all he knew and loved, he could only ask, "How could this be?" As he walked farther, his head sagged toward the ground. He said to himself, "Catholics and Protestants both laid claim to the same God, the one who taught forgiveness, reconciliation, and peace! Where is it?" He shook his head and trudged on.

He walked past where the wharf had been before it burned, to go to the seashore. It seemed to him this was the sole remnant of stability and continuity in his life. The rhythm of the waves calmed him. He was in hopes of finding a fragile, white, hinged-shell like the one he had so carefully selected six years before. He wanted to replace the original that met its end when the first baby grabbed it from Madelaine's neck. He found none; every shell was split or broken.

Childhood failure had originally humiliated him. Now the actions of people in his new religion caused him as much guilt and humiliation. This alone was so overpowering, he could hardly put one foot in front of the other. As the sun set over the water, he started back toward their street. An occasional stray dog sniffed through the cooling rubble for something to eat. In the distance, he saw a few people. They may also have been looking for their families. No one dared ask.

Dusk shrouded the eerie scene at the Germaine home. The vengeance of the dragonnades was obvious. Apparently they had forced entry into the home and killed everyone inside. The terrible stench told him they had set fire to the bodies. The only vestiges of family life were an iron hinge and door latch that lay at his feet and the black andirons that had cradled wood in their fireplace.

His shoulders drooped in his desperate, angry grief as he tried to hold back his tears. He could not. Dreams of life in America had already failed. Dreams of life in France were getting more tortured by the day.

Pierre harnessed the donkey to the wooden-wheeled cart and turned it around to head up the hillside. Under protection of darkness he started for St. Felix. Traveling was slow at any time. Progress was painfully slow with the donkey at his side.

Madelaine had been anxiously waiting for Pierre's return. She knew it would take two days each way for Pierre to walk there and back, but now more than five days had passed and there was no sign of him. She had warmed his meal several nights in anticipation of his arrival, but still he had not come.

She was in the depths of exhausted sleep, a twin on each side when she was startled by the familiar creaking sounds of the donkey cart. When she jumped up from the straw mat the babies awoke crying. By the time Pierre came through the door there was a din of noise. He had hoped his quiet footsteps would have avoided this chaos.

The light from the bullrush lamp shone on his face as he entered, soot covered, weary, and sad. He couldn't utter a word. Just seeing him shake his head, Madelaine knew. She did not want to hear.

The message Madelaine asked Nicole to write next, was the saddest of all.

Dear Charles, Terrible tragedy. Draggonades burned house. Family killed. Am very sad and tired. Don't know if I can go on. M.

In the weeks that followed, Pierre became more and more concerned about Madelaine. She lay on the straw mat much of the day, able to do nothing more than nurse the babies. She was too weak to sit up. It was hot that summer, but she shivered day and night, despite the extra woolens Nicole brought from her house. Madelaine stopped eating. She cried all night.

Pierre was beside himself. He asked Nicole and her husband for further help. Already Nicole had tried by stealing eggs plus scraps of meat and fat from the plates at the Manor House. Nothing interested Madelaine. Not even smiles from her older children could make their mother's face brighten.

She rarely spoke. She could only lament how she had betrayed the cause of the Huguenots and the Germaine family in particular. She convinced herself, that her family's tragedy had been a direct result of having abandoned her Protestant faith.

Pierre worried she would never come out of this state of despair. If she didn't start eating soon, not only would he lose his wife, but the twins would starve.

Chapter 14

Nicole the Problem-solver

As the sun rose over the flax fields, it cast a shadow on the sundial mounted beside the door of the field-master's cottage at the foot of the hill closest to the Manor House. Soon the men would gather to hear the orders of the day.

When the field master came into the field, it signaled the end of a long work day. He would measure the size of their bundles, tied as specified for shipping and check off each man's harvest that day against his pre-set seasonal quota for the Lord. Any yield beyond that was theirs.

The field master seldom yelled, but a stern command told the field hands when they better shape up, work faster, or stay later. After all, he spoke for the Lord of the Manor whom they had seldom seen.

For the past two years the balance of sun and rain had produced bumper crops. Nicole's husband had brought home a goodly amount that had exceeded his quota. Lengths of yardage were also part of the quota for some families.

Various options were open to families to earn extra money. The men could sell the bundles of raw flax to the Lord, or bring it home for their wives. The women could go through the lengthy process of retting the stalks to rot the outer shield as was necessary before these long strands could be transformed into thread at their spinning wheels.

One option would then be to prepare measured lengths of this thread to wind onto their looms so that it would yield the standard length of 12 yards of fabric. Threads woven for garments were finer than the sturdy, coarse version they made into sailcloth canvas.

The Lord of the Manor would market their products, along with his own, in Bordeaux. Of these various products, it was weaving the sailcloth that gave the women the most pride and power, elevating their feelings of self-worth. It created a firm bond among them. One expressed their empowerment this way, "If we can't go to America, we can make the sailcloth so others can."

Women who set up their looms with heavy thread to weave the canvas seldom wove anything else. Whereas it was costly for them to buy the required indigo-dyed thread that characterized sailcloth worldwide, the product they made was more lucrative at market. Weavers were precise in setting up their looms. The two adjacent blue threads had to be placed one inch from the left and right selvage edges in all sailcloth. This guided the sail-maker's needle.

Just as lucrative were the very fine linen strands that other women spun. They were wound in a continuous thread around a barrel near the top, in sets of 10 rounds and then tied. Few of them could count any further, but they could tie 10 threads in sets of 10. They lifted these fine threads carefully to twist into a skein. These would be shipped from Bordeaux to Antwerp for the lace-makers. The nuns there were known for the fine laces they made that would adorn the clothes of rich burgers in Amsterdam.

Regrettably, the wives who specialized in spinning the fine threads for lace making did not feel the same pride and camaraderie as the weavers of sailcloth. They had no clue about the lace-makers of Antwerp, nor how those who wore the laces looked in their costly finery. All they understood was the unglamorous task of producing high-quality thread from the raw material their husbands labored hard to produce in the fields.

Nicole's loom was set up to make sailcloth, whereas Madelaine's provided yardage for family needs and rarely did she have extra lengths to sell to the Lord of the Manor. Compared to Madelaine's tall, slender stature, Nicole was broad shouldered and heavy set. Seldom did she run out of energy.

It was Nicole who hoisted heavy rolls of sailcloth over her shoulder to lug up the long hill. This, and each of the other products the women made to sell were brought to the Manor House for the Lord to inspect before he purchased it as middleman between them and the wholesalers in Bordeaux.

The wives relied on Nicole to advise them as to what was bringing the best prices. In return for handling their products, they gave her the equivalent of a yard for every 12-yard length, or a suitable number of skeins she calculated at the end of the season.

Indeed, Nicole was looked up to by all the wives for her various talents. Who but Nicole had ever been to the Manor House or had seen how they lived? She became their authority on most matters.

It was rumored in the field one year that the price of flax at the docks had gone up. Thus, Nicole felt that the wives should get more for their wares. They were amazed to hear that she dared to ask a higher price of the Lord of the Manor. They were shocked even more that she got it!

Only then did the field master advocate a better rate for the bundles the workers harvested in his fields. Nicole's talents had been clearly recognized by the wives, but the husbands were slow to acknowledge them—that is, until now.

What Nicole enjoyed most was the role she envisioned as a power-broker. Since the price of flax had increased, she told the Lord of the Manor that the quota of yardage the wives were obliged to provide for their quota should be reduced accordingly. The women were overjoyed. Their husbands were shocked out of their minds. Some even feared she had gone too far.

Even though Nicole's husband was 10 years older, it was she who was in charge at home. It may have been due to the fact her previous role as aunt had changed to mother so fast following her sister's death. On the other hand, this dominant trait may have been inherent in her family's background.

Her parents had moved from the coal-mining Alsace region on the eastern edge of France that bordered Germany. Over the generations, these hardy miners had seen the Alsace aligned alternately with France and Germany. Their French dialect was colored by a harsh accent. When Nicole was upset with her husband this accent was very apparent. It could have given her the self-confidence she needed when she negotiated prices with the Lord of the Manor as well.

Her husband's oldest son had married at 17. He now lived several miles away but continued to work at the Manor House caring for the horses. Her husband's other two boys were old enough to help in the fields. This increased the amount of raw flax they could call their own. By standards of the time their family was clearly moving up. Nicole intended to stay on this path.

While Pierre looked up to both Nicole and her husband for help and advice, he knew instinctively that Nicole was the real problem-solver. He discussed with them how worried he was about Madelaine and how desperate he was to do something.

The only relief he could think of for Madelaine would be to help her rescue Charles, but that seemed to be out of the question. Ever since his capture they had all tried to dream up a plausible plan for his escape. Making water run up hill would have been just as likely.

For more than a month Madelaine had scarcely eaten. Now her survival was as crucial as her brother's. Pierre worried because the twins were already losing weight. "How much longer can she last?" With his large, sturdy hands covering his face, he cried, "I could lose one, two, or all three of them."

Nicole too feared for the life of her best friend. Even though she had already been stealing fat and table scraps as well as eggs for Madelaine nothing had stirred her appetite.

One day while Nicole was working up at the big house, an idea flashed across her mind. She was dusting the room where she and her husband had watched the Lord make his signature. She got so excited with this revolutionary solution she dropped a delicate china teacup, something she had never done before. Fortunately it hit the rug and didn't break.

Back at home that afternoon she waited and watched. It seemed like forever before the men came out of the fields. Finally they headed home tired and dirty.

"Why do they just saunter?" She wanted to run to meet them, but she knew she shouldn't. If she had, they would fear she had bad news about Madelaine or the twins. All she could do was wait as usual, outside her cottage.

Restraining her excitement more than she wanted to, she managed to speak to Pierre before he reached his cottage. "Pierre, why don't you come over this evening?"

Later, when he arrived she ushered him into her cottage where her husband, Etienne, was waiting. "Sit down right here."

As much as she had expected to lay out her startling idea calmly, she heard herself blurting out, "Pierre, you have your paper!"

Pierre stiffened.

Nicole realized she must have frightened him with her Alsatian accent. Of course, that would mystify him, for he had owned his plot for over a year. Even though this event had been important, she was sure he couldn't see how that related to their present situation. He could be forgiven for not recognizing any hint of the steps that Nicole envisioned for all of them.

"Don't you see? You could sell your piece of paper to us!" She realized that neither man had any idea of what she really meant by this. "And then you could move your family to La Tremblade. At least Madelaine would feel closer to Charles, even if she couldn't see him."

Pierre simply stared at her.

Nicole's husband remained quiet. Nicole understood it would take him more time to process it all and to feel he was a part of this complex plan that would be important to his family's welfare, too.

Pierre smiled as he grasped the potential of the whole idea. "Yes, yes. This could work. We would have to work long and hard, but we could do this. We have Don-the-Donkey to help us move the family. Finally, that old donkey will be of use."

To make it all work would take faith—faith they knew as generational Huguenots and faith now, as the New Catholics that they were.

Chapter 15

The Plan

Pierre returned to his cottage that night, deep in thought. Madelaine lay on their straw mat, her face to the wall. Was she asleep or not? These days it was hard to tell. He watched, to be sure she was breathing.

He knew he needed time to mull over in his mind all he wanted to tell her. He decided to wait another day or two. Maybe Sunday would be best, when he didn't have to work. Then he planned to feed it to her in small pieces she could accept. Otherwise the magnitude of the venture could be overpowering. As weak as she was, she would feel she scarcely had energy to do anything. It would be daunting, to realize what each of them would have to do for the whole plan to succeed.

At times it seemed to Pierre that this entire idea seemed too risky to even consider, but he was desperate to save the lives of his family. He had no choice. Just as he had to feed the idea to Madelaine in small bits he would deal with the enormity of it himself piece by piece.

The morning after Pierre had learned of Nicole's idea, he was still pre-occupied with all that lay ahead. As he was dressing to go to work, he looked down, chagrined. His pants were on backwards.

Just the idea of moving closer to Charles gave Madelaine the glimmer of hope she needed. She began to eat the table scraps Nicole brought. Best of all she liked the eggs Nicole "lifted" on her detour through the barnyard. Nicole didn't consider it was stealing unless she took them from the house. When she found one lying where the hen had laid it, she considered it a "gift."

As Madelaine began to gain strength, she sat up to nurse the babies and watch her older children with greater interest. No longer did she become as angry with Jeanne, now 3½, when occasionally she insisted that she needed attention, too.

The summer of 1686 was long and warm and again the men reaped a third harvest of flax. By now the twins were six months old and Charles had been in prison for a year. Soon after she learned of Charles' capture, Madelaine would lie awake nights fantasizing a range of solutions to free him. None was feasible, given the dire circumstances, but that didn't keep her from trying. One fantasy in particular kept recurring. It was only Nicole with whom she shared this daring idea. Nicole told Madelaine she was often reminded of this on her way to church services when she passed the monks weeding their gardens.

Now that they had a broader plan in mind, this long-standing fantasy of Madelaine's seemed to fit right in. But implementing such a complex plan seemed preposterous at times even to Nicole, but she never let on. Any doubts, any hesitation, could sabotage hopes of rescuing Charles and the momentum it would take to execute it.

Madelaine was soon strong enough to envision how she would carry out her specific role. Wild as this plan was, it began to seem plausible to both of them. Nicole reasoned that given enough time, Madelaine would be up to the task both physically and mentally. To bolster Madelaine's confidence Nicole took it upon herself to begin the first step.

One afternoon as Nicole was leaving her work at the Manor House, she detoured to the horse barn to speak with her oldest step-son. With a sense of eagerness in her voice, she said: "You go to that place in your town where they dye thread and— You hear me? You get me some dark brown dye." The young man leaned against a stall and stared at his muck-covered shoes. He needed more urging. "You know the place, it's where they dye the indigo threads I use to weave sailcloth."

His voice sagged as much as his slender frame, as he replied,

"Why would you need brown dye?"

Thinking fast, she replied: "I like to have variety. Don't want to do the same thing all my life." Nicole knew that such a thought would never occur to this young man, since neither his father, nor anyone else he knew ever varied from a set life-path. He expected no different in his, so this came to him as a startling idea no matter what the reason was that Nicole wanted the dye. He rolled his eyes in doubt but Nicole knew he would comply with her demand for several reasons. He liked her, and he knew she loved and cared about all of them, bringing them up as she did, quite literally on instant demand.

"And don't let them ask you any questions. It's none of their business what we make. They don't know what will sell in Bordeaux," she added to keep him off track and silence any further questions. On second thought, her mention of Bordeaux may not have been so smart.

Nicole ran down the hill from the Manor House late one afternoon, and burst into Madelaine's house, panting from exertion. "I've got it!"

Madelaine struggled up from her rocker. "What have you got?"

"The brown dye we'll need!"

"Brown dye? What for?"

"What do you mean, what for? For the robe."

"Oh? I thought monks wore white robes."

"You're thinking of priests. They wear white, and I hear the Pope does, too." Although Nicole had converted to Catholicism only a few years before, she readily assumed her position as an authority on church matters. "Well, maybe there are monks who wear white, but we're going to make him a Franciscan."

"Oh, all right, whatever you think is best." Madelaine still wasn't sure what Nicole's actual plan was since she had no knowledge of the workings of the Catholic church.

"Anyway, with brown, it is easier to keep a low profile, and a hooded monk will have an added advantage of disguise."

Motivated by each of Nicole's enterprising moves, Madelaine grew more convinced that this scheme might really work. It had taken Nicole's tremendous effort, planning, and cunning to bring together all they had to be done, but that was what she did best!

As part of this plan, Nicole carefully chose thread that would be the right weight for the new warp on Madelaine's loom. These threads were somewhat softer than she used for sailcloth, but not as fine as those Madelaine wove into cloth for family use. Then Nicole had to scurry around among the neighbors to collect enough skeins that would match. She had to do this without arousing unwanted questions. Nicole knew the threat this posed to her, to her livelihood, and to her family—in addition to risking failure of the overall scheme.

There was a strong chance that rumors might start that were harder to quell than a wild fire. She couldn't burden Madelaine with her worries, she had to shoulder these alone. Neither of their husbands knew of this aspect of the plan. Even if they had known, they could hardly have put themselves in her shoes to provide suitable support. She would have to rely on her stalwart Alsatian background to fortify herself against fears that were only too real.

The wives had always depended on her and trusted her to act fairly on their behalf when she took their goods to the Manor House to sell. Now, if they suspected in any way that she was gathering all these skeins for more lucrative sales in Bordeaux without telling them, their trust in her could be doomed, her power-base lost forever. She could be seen as an untrustworthy conniver in their eyes!

Fears aside, once she had enough matched skeins of thread, she would have no trouble re-warping Madelaine's loom. The big challenge was the intervening step. She had never watched anyone dye thread, so she had to rely on her own devices and carry it out while shielded from prying eyes. Since their own

cottages were at the end, the adjacent woods were an advantage. They could hide behind the donkey cart and the donkey hitched to a low branch.

After each skein had taken on the deep brown color she wanted, Nicole hung them one by one to dry on a branch deep in the woods sharing a gleeful grin with Madelaine as she did so. It was just as important for Madelaine to once again enjoy life as it was to succeed in this act that was intrinsic to the goal itself.

Soon Nicole was ready to measure out lengths of thread to re-warp the loom, while Madelaine sat in her rocker to nurse the babies. When Pierre came home that night and saw brown threads on her loom for the very first time he was puzzled. "What in heaven's name is going on?" Nicole hurried over to support Madelaine and reinforce in Pierre's mind, what a dramatic piece in the puzzle, this warp of deep brown signified.

It was only then they shared the meaning of this and other pieces of the puzzle yet to unfold. Pierre shouldn't have been so surprised, knowing how enterprising each of these women could be. While he was justifiably impressed by their innovative thinking, it made his stomach flip, as he sensed the unknown future edging closer.

Madelaine began to envision more details of their unique plan step by step. This alone was therapeutic, except for those moments when it seemed too complex and overwhelming. But try they must. What other options did they have?

Madelaine spent every spare moment at her loom. She looked from her weaving, to the cradle and smiled to see these young things beginning to grow.

Months passed and the brown warp was gradually transformed into their treasured, special yardage and protected from the knowledge of neighbors.

Before the little ones were old enough to pull themselves up Madelaine moved her loom against the wall beside the door to protect the warp threads from their grasp as well as she could. Also she could keep an eye on Jeanne playing outside near the oven. She loved to play Mommy with her doll-size loaves of bread.

When Madelaine was weaving and Jeanne wanted attention, she would let her daughter sit on her lap and hold her little hand to push the shuttle wound with *weft* thread, sometimes called *woof*, through the wedge-shaped opening of warp threads. When the twins were demanding her mother's full attention, Jeanne would compete by tickling her mother's foot as she shifted it from one pedal to the other.

Joseph was the precocious one, climbing up one side of the weaving bench, onto his mother's back and across to the other side. When she wasn't weaving, he would climb up the side of the loom, balancing as if gravity had no effect on him.

Mary was content to sit nearby on the floor, playing with a shuttle full of thread. When she held it out too far, she easily lost her balance and toppled over.

Madelaine could be the most productive when the twins slept but that was when she wanted more than anything to take a nap, too. Amid these distractions, the fabric grew inch by inch, and yard by yard. As she pulled the loom's beater back to beat each thread into place, Madelaine felt more intense joy in the process than ever before. She leaned back to admire her work. The possibility of achieving their goal improved day by day through the work of her very own hands. Madelaine was confident she could fully implement her part, the part she had dreamed of so long; now presumably there was a means of carrying it out. Passing her fingers across the cloth, she often felt as though it was Charles she was touching.

For the first time since she had heard of her family's tragic end she began to feel like herself. No longer did she feel so chilled. Her heart warmed her from within. Holding a baby in each arm, she rocked them to sleep, singing softly, "Frere Jacques, Frere Jacques, dormez-vous? Dormez-vous?"

"Nicole, it's time to send another message to Charles." She thought for a moment, before she could fully express her thoughts. "Tell him the flax crop is good, and I am weaving hard. Most of all, he is to keep the faith." While she knew the reference to her weaving would have no significance for him it was important to her.

Nicole was excited that her scheme was having such a positive effect. She brought over bountiful armloads of raw flax as partial payment for the cottage. Together they carried these to the nearby stream where they would leave the rigid flax stems to *ret* or rot for a few months. After stripping the softened protective covering from the long fibers, Madelaine twisted the soft strands between her thumb and fingers at the spinning wheel.

As she completed weaving the yardage on the brown warp, she said a grateful prayer for success this far, and an ardent plea for God's help to complete the plan. She removed the treasured fabric and folded it carefully for its anticipated use. Then she re-warped her loom to weave the customary yardage her family would need for next season's clothing, yardage they would not need to hide from curious eyes.

Chapter 16

Path to the Future

It had been but two months since Nicole had floated her ambitious solution when this incident occurred. Madelaine's fantasy was beginning to take shape, but she still worried.

Predictable moments of silence punctuated rumbling trouths of Pierre's deep sleep, while Madelaine was wide awake, pondering the imponderables. As her strength increased, she could begin to recognize how many unknowns might lay ahead.

Anxious to discuss her concerns, she shook Pierre awake. He responded with a disgruntled "Huh...Un-huh," and went back to sleep. The next morning he asked what she had been trying to tell him that was so urgent.

As fervently as she hoped their plans would materialize, her concerns for a safe future often churned in her mind at night. She worried whether Charles' rescue was even possible, but that was way off in the distance. More urgent was her worry over the four little ones, as they would be leaving their known surroundings to travel into the unknown that lay ahead.

"Pierre, we can't just start out without knowing whether we can even make it. It's too big a risk. We have to know you will have work. And that we'll have a place to live with all these little ones?"

He didn't disagree but he didn't rush to do what he knew in his own mind had to be done. It would take courage and a sound night's sleep to approach the field master. Under the pretense of distress about an "imaginary" family who desperately needed his help, he presented a duly saddened expression.

With serious trepidation he bid his wife farewell and set

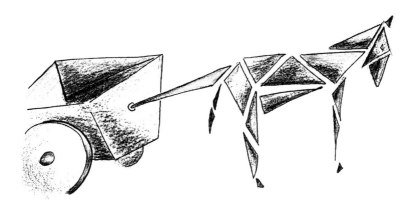

out to walk to La Tremblade. Then he could see for himself whether they could possibly carry out this wild but essential mission.

Unknowns petrified him. It seemed that he was looking into a deep, treacherous abyss. From the unconscious, a clear image erupted of his clutching the rope ladder.

Along this journey he would, of course, have to rely on the good graces of Huguenots. He prayed they would not reject him for having converted to Catholicism. Over these 45 miles, Pierre was quietly passed from house to house. Later these would provide way-stations where his family could rest. Although he could walk 10 to 15 miles a day along footpaths, he knew it would take much longer for the donkey cart loaded with children and belongings to travel that far.

Stubborn as the donkey was, Pierre knew that when the time came, he would be grateful to have him and the wooden cart to move his family. The Germaine family in La Rochelle had named him Don Juan, but in St. Felix he was spoken of in loving terms as Don-the-Donkey. Never had he shared their motivation to move, nor would he now. Pierre worried about complications the donkey would impose during the family's long journey.

Pierre tried to envision how he might try to urge him to move one hoof in front of the other. Perhaps if someone walked ahead with a handful of straw he would move. If that didn't work, maybe the shrill cries of the little ones would hurt his ears so much he would move in a fruitless effort to distance himself from them.

For now Pierre had to put aside the problems he would have to face during the later trip to focus his energy on this one. Once families learned it was someone from the Germaine family who needed help, they willingly offered him assistance and provided him a signal to indicate to other families he would meet, to do so as well.

The family name was instantly recognizable. Those who had remained Huguenots, and others who had been forced to convert for their survival, were ready to help. They offered to provide shelter, food, and support both now, and when he returned with his family. Often they would inquire about what had happened in La Rochelle in general and to the Germaine family in particular.

A family in La Tremblade not only took Pierre in, they offered to arrange shelter when he returned with his family. The locals had chosen this family among the New Catholics because the head of the family worked at the prison. Through the courageous endeavors of this former Huguenot he arranged for Pierre to be employed as a prison guard when he returned. It was more than he could have hoped for.

Pierre reasoned to himself, converting to Catholicism had its drawbacks. However, if there was to be any advantage, he felt entitled to make use of it. But he would also discover there would be unanticipated issues in his new job.

The return trip to St. Felix was faster. He was anxious to be back with Madelaine and the little ones. Pierre reasoned, and rightly so, that realistically it would take another year before their move could actually happen. There was so much for each of them to do it would take that long and by then his precipitous absence would be forgotten. They could proceed in plain sight with part of the tasks such as collecting an extra large crop of flax by Nicole's family to pay for Pierre's plot. Other steps had to be done surreptitiously so as not to arouse suspicions of neighbors or the Lord of the Manor. Too much was at stake!

Be that as it may, he had laid the groundwork for their trip and a future that could enable them to execute their strategy. His mind returned to his young family as he walked along the dirt path. He tried to envision how the twins would be 18 months old by then, Jeanne would be 4½, and Jacques would be nearly 7 years old.

Chapter 17

Writing Lessons

The year that followed Pierre's trip to La Tremblade had been filled with hard work for all of them. Nicole and her family worked furiously to reap a bigger harvest. Nicole wove extra yards of sailcloth for part of the payment for the cottage and Madelaine had completed her responsibility by late spring. Now it was up to the men. Neither had a clue about the task Nicole had in store for them but she was undeterred. In fact, she reveled in the thought as she carried her weaving bench out the door, past Madelaine's cottage and around the corner.

"Can't be too careful, Pierre," she said as she set it down in front of him. "Never know when kids or their parents' nosey eyes will turn into wagging tongues." She went back for the piece of crude paper she had saved from the Manor House for this special occasion.

She was glad she had their papers of ownership from which to copy each name so that she could create the final document herself. She stopped at Madelaine's to watch her meticulously remove Pierre's paper one corner at a time, from above the fireplace. It had been stuck there with daubs of honey since shortly before the twins were born.

Madelaine handed the paper to Nicole with a confident, expectant smile, but Nicole blanched. There in bold block letters was his Huguenot name. Now he was Pierre Anton. How could she manage that? She had nothing to pattern his new name after.

It didn't take long before a broad smile crossed her face. She recalled with humor that Pierre had "made up" his own name. "So, Madelaine, if there is no family and he doesn't know how to spell his name, how would anyone else know?" She felt confident that this freed her to do whatever she had to do.

Around the corner of Madelaine's cottage near the weaving bench, Nicole sharpened several turkey quills against a rock. One by one, she dipped them into the dried gourd that contained the small residual of boiled stamen powder. Fearful the round-bottom gourd would be easily knocked over on the weaving bench, she put it on the ground and stabilized it with a few stones.

Pierre dropped to his knees at the weaving bench for his first lesson. He watched Nicole carefully print PIERRE ANTON in two-inch letters for him to trace. She showed him where to start each letter and handed him the pen. Another time she would expect him to trace a smaller version. Later he would print it from memory. Not only was printing a stepping stone to writing his signature, she thought he should be able to recognize his name on anything he might have to sign.

Pierre had to concentrate so hard he soon grew too tired to continue. He was thankful for once that his name was no longer La Fountaine. He envisioned how that could be twice as difficult, or at least twice as long.

Nicole's husband was next. She turned the piece of crude paper over and printed out ETIENNE La FARGE. Etienne had heard that he would be called Stephen in America. "Would that be easier to write?" he wondered. He let go of the thought as he dropped to his knees to face what would be a formidable task.

He had watched as Pierre struggled. To be sure, it was harder still for him. His hands were 10 years older, stiff, and puffy from clutching big clumps of flax. His fingers weren't at all accustomed to holding the straw-like slippery turkey quill Nicole had sharpened. Worse yet, he had to form minute, sequential motions precisely as Nicole directed. In a barely audible voice, he grumbled: "A day's work under the field master is easier than this."

Being summer solstice, they had plenty of time to practice as it was light until nearly 11. They all relished these long evenings although it was hard to get the children to call it a day. The sky never got pitch black in late June and early July. Dawn began at 4 a.m.

Nicole held her writing lessons over several weeks whenever the men weren't too tired from working extra hours in good light. Gradually they were finding it easier to direct their clumsy fingers. Even though the Lord of the Manor had accepted an X as legal, Nicole felt she could take no such chance. Only their signatures would do.

She improvised wavy, curving lines for each one's first and last names just like the Lord had done when he signed his name. What had impressed her most was how rapidly he had written it. She would expect no less from them, as lords of their own manors.

Nicole prepared a signature for each of them to copy, first in large size, then small. They struggled, but gradually they began to master the task in bits, then all of it. Nicole turned the paper over for each to do from memory. Success! Etienne had been ever so proud. He radiated joy. Nicole had never seen him this way. She was just as proud. It would have been reward enough for all their efforts to see these hard-earned signatures materialize, even if there was to be no transfer of land.

As the men worked side by side, they were ever so cautious not to let a word of their intent slip. During the last afternoon Nicole practiced her part in great anticipation. She arranged the spacing of their names and the lettering just as it would appear on the "real" document. The night of the big event was full of heightened excitement they dared not share.

Trying to keep everything routine, each family ate the evening meal in customary fashion. After the children were asleep, Madelaine took down their paper from above the fireplace for the last time. Nicole would have to work around the sticky spots on the back to prepare this new document, a document that could be properly recognized by anyone in the future. Never before had she felt such power. She loved it.

The event would be both joyful and tearful. Most of all, this was one of the most significant benchmarks in the long step-by-step process toward their ultimate goal. For Madelaine, this step provided necessary mobility for her family and, hopefully the rescue of her brother. For Nicole, it meant her family would acquire another piece of land and an assurance of grandchildren nearby, the first of whom was expected in the fall. Mentally, Nicole gave herself a well-deserved pat on the back for having devised this scheme that was working so far.

Knowing how excited Nicole was to have her stepson and family next door, Madelaine was surprised that they weren't there to watch.

"Oh, no, I couldn't risk it. I don't know his wife that well. She might tell." She inhaled a deep breath. "Can't let a word leak to the Manor House." They stole a sly glance at each other, knowing that the Lord of the Manor was losing a reliable worker who, for the past seven years, had helped pad his pockets in Bordeaux. Nicole acknowledged to Madelaine her fear that when he heard what had happened he might feel justified in reclaiming Pierre's plot. She whispered, "If the paper was legal the first time, it should be legal now, with signatures to prove it." Madelaine was amazed to see how Nicole could think so far ahead.

Madelaine wondered if ever again she would have such a close friend, and one she could look up to as much for all her sharp thinking and keen ideas. She could hardly keep from shedding tears of sorrow that soon would be mingled in tears of joy.

First it was Nicole who knelt at the weaving bench. She prepared the proper format, printing each name, and very carefully designating the "from" and "to" columns. Above each printed name she drew a line for them to place their well-practiced signatures.

Beneath her husband's name, Nicole decided to add her own. If she couldn't own land, she felt entitled to be a joint partner in this important venture. As she prepared to print it,

she suddenly realized she had never seen letters that stood for "Nicole" but nothing daunted her now, with her experience in improvising.

When Nicole finished preparing the final document on this parchment paper, she stood up. It was quite unheard of for anyone other than Kings or Lords to own property. Nicole felt justifiably proud that now they would own property even beyond their cottage footprint. She threw her shoulders back, put her hands on her hips and smiled with satisfaction. With those magical strokes of a quill pen, they would be land owners in the absolute sense.

The final moment was at hand. First Pierre knelt to make his signature in the right place. Madelaine watched closely. She felt her heart beat so hard, it seemed that the Catholic cross she was wearing vibrated on her chest. After Etienne had struggled to keep his signature on the line, Nicole added hers. It was only then that Madelaine felt it was the real moment, that mysterious moment, that signaled the land beneath her feet had actually been transferred. For her, a seismic event could not have been more momentous.

Even the men's eyes glazed over when they sensed the full contractual meaning of this event. Sadly, it also meant a final goodbye. Never again would the couples be together, nor wrap their arms around each other, to share warm tears.

Chapter 18

Moving by Donkey Cart

Never could Pierre and Madelaine have dreamed of acquiring a donkey and donkey cart on their own. Don Juan was an important legacy, the only one, that emerged from the terrible tragedy in La Rochelle. Surprisingly it would be Don-the-Donkey who would carry forth the religious and cultural history for unborn generations of the Germaine family.

Recently, Don-the-Donkey had been the principal curiosity of 18-month-old Joseph. Being the precocious climber that he was at such a young age, his mother smiled and mused whether he may have inherited this trait from his Uncle Charles. He tried to get onto the sleeping donkey's back from the low branch where he was hitched. The donkey's eyes opened then.

With the land having been properly transferred as dusk fell, all was in order for the next step. Darkness cloaked Pierre's actions as he hitched the donkey to the cart. They disassembled the loom and loaded all their possessions. Straw mats would cushion the ride for the children. Their mother planned to sit beside them on her weaving bench. She left the cradle for the new occupants in hopes she wouldn't need it again.

By midnight, Pierre was ready to carry the sleeping children out one by one and hand them up to Madelaine in the cart. Suddenly she cried in a loud whisper, "Wait a minute! I need to do something else first."

"What," Pierre wondered, "could be so important now?" He waited by the cart growing more impatient because they weren't starting when he expected. With the nights being so short, time was critical to safeguard their departure. "What could be more important than that?" He wanted to know, but he dared not speak out loud.

Madelaine rushed around to the front of the cottage, to her special spot at the end of the flax field and knelt in silence. She patted the ground for the last time. Tears rolled down her cheeks and vanished into the soil. Reluctantly she got up.

Madelaine climbed into the cart and Pierre lifted the children up to her one by one. Jacques and Jeanne barely woke up and the twins slept until the cart began to move. Madelaine quickly muffled their cries with the heavy, brown garment she had fashioned in just the right way for its future mission.

Pierre winced as the cart creaked louder than ever under this load. Don-the-Donkey was doubly reluctant. Nevertheless Pierre was able to get moving soon after the peak of darkness. From the far end of the flax fields he stopped briefly to listen before moving on.

No one from the row of cottages seemed to have been aroused. Good! Their departure would be evident at dawn, when the men assembled by the sundial for their orders. Nicole's husband, Etienne, would maintain that he had heard nothing.

After Madelaine had looked back toward the cottages, she was overwhelmed by the prospect of losing her deep friendship with Nicole as well as the treasure she had buried. In the next moment she cried out in a loud whisper, "Pierre! Stop! Stop the cart!"

"We can't stop now, it's too risky!" That didn't deter her. She stood up while the cart was still in motion, stepped onto the rolling axle, jumped off and disappeared into the darkness.

"What are you doing? Are you out of your mind?" But Madelaine was beyond the audible range of his whispered pleas.

Her heart was pounding when she reached the special spot. It took but a moment to find it in the dark and push away the loose dirt. Then she stood up and raced back to the cart.

Pierre was taken by complete surprise. Immediately he recognized the shape of the Huguenot cross. He understood how hard it would be to leave this behind, but he feared it presented an added risk, should it be found on them. Madelaine disregarded his concern for she already knew where she would hide it. Mary was toilet trained. Joseph wasn't. A smile crossed her face as she reasoned that he could provide the perfect place.

Anxious to get as far as possible from the clutches of the Lord of the Manor before dawn rose at 4 o'clock, Pierre urged the donkey to increase his pace. Little changed. Traveling at night was easier in some respects. The babies were more apt to sleep.

At daybreak Madelaine discovered that, slow as the donkey was, this motion was unsettling to the children. They were affected first one by one, then all at the same time. They wanted to get out of the cart, but only Jacques could be depended on to walk beside his father, and then he soon tired.

When they were going uphill, Madelaine walked to lighten the load, and the twins insisted on getting out too. They were apt to take off in opposite directions so Jacques and Jeanne, were charged with helping to keep them under control.

No sooner was Joseph lifted back into the cart on one side, than he was planning his escape from the other. This frustrated Pierre so much he wondered whether Joseph and Don-the-Donkey had an unspoken conspiracy between them. It was sometimes easier at night when the donkey was unable to see the long trail ahead.

Madelaine had plenty of time for her own thoughts. She hoped their new home would have planked floors like those of her childhood. Then perhaps the children wouldn't suffer those eternal colds. She doctored them the best she could by preparing flaxseed poultices for Jeanne's feverish chest and boiled flaxseed to a yellowed, lumpy, gelatinous mass to ease her throat. When she had a lump of sugar or honey to add, this attracted all of them.

Now that they were far enough from the clutches of the Manor House to be safe, they could travel in daylight as bonafide Catholics on the move. At noon on the fourth day they stopped to eat by a cool fast-running stream. In fact it was very cold! Water from the Rhone Glacier on the Swiss border rushed past to empty into the broad Gironde estuary some called a river, that linked the port of Bordeaux with the Atlantic Ocean.

Pierre unhooked the cart so he could lead Don-the-Donkey to the cold stream. It was the best part of the trip for the donkey. He could cool his hoofs and take much-needed drinks of fresh water. He deserved it all.

The children delighted in wading in the cold shallow water. They sprayed each other and gave chase in screams and giggles.

Madelaine prepared what was left of the food for their lunch. Gone were the hard-boiled eggs Nicole had prepared for them, gifts of the barnyard hens, and the tasty round of cheese she had liberated from the Manor House kitchen. Only the four-day-old bread remained. It was among the extra loaves Madelaine had baked the day they left, and cautiously taken around the corner of the cottage to cool. The crust was so hard, it took Pierre's strong hands to break it open so the little ones could dig out the interior.

Day lilies bloomed in profusion along the path. Jeanne picked a bouquet of bright yellow mustard blossoms and day lilies for her mother. It was the orange day lilies that little Mary grabbed with both hands. The brown powdery stamens soon decorated her face, her fingers, and her sister. Everyone laughed. They were cleaned up in the stream before climbing back into the cart for the final two-hour leg of the trip.

As they neared La Tremblade Madelaine began to smell the salty sea breeze. Only two or three miles away was the coastal town of Place de La Coubre, the same La Coubre that had spelled the tragic end for members of the crew of *L'Esprit*.

Seagulls shrieked their constant welcome—or complaints, who could tell. "Caw...Caw...Caw..." Madelaine and Pierre exchanged fond glances, at the sounds and the smells that brought back memories of La Rochelle. Only now, could they acknowledge to themselves and each other how much they had missed it during the seven years they had lived in St. Felix.

112

With all the duress that the very word La Tremblade had represented in their lives the past two years, living near the coast could have its bright spots, or so they hoped, if their mission could be accomplished. That was yet to be seen. Success or failure weighed equally. On second thought perhaps failure weighed even more heavily.

Much as Madelaine was heartened by the signs of the seacoast she loved, the first sight of the prison devastated her. Cold stone was impenetrable from without, disheartening within. Her hopes started to fade. After all the effort of the past year, to now be faced with grim reality made her begin to lose faith in their plan.

Was Charles even alive? He could have been dead that whole time and they would have no way of knowing. Letters that Nicole had prepared were as important for Madelaine to keep up her hope, as they were for her brother if he ever received them.

Madelaine realized that the steps they had taken over the past year, hard as they had been, were remarkably successful. She reviewed in her mind how Nicole had originated the scheme, taught the men to sign their names, purchased their cottage with bundles of flax and yards of cloth, plus she provided food for the trip from the barnyard and the Manor House kitchen. What remarkable feats! What a truly remarkable friend!

Now it would be up to Pierre to carry the ball. Madelaine had faith in him now, just as she had had in their youth at the time when he had lost so much faith in himself. But he must not fail this time! A life depended on him. If he succeeded he would fulfill his wife's expectations, but if any part of this ingenious plan began to unravel he would forever feel at fault.

Like Madelaine, Pierre too, hated to leave the home they had built together. More than that he was feeling increased anxiety about the future. The closer they got, the more often Pierre walked with his head lowered, deep in thought. He was moving to a new job. It was scary because he had never done anything but work in the fields. His large, chunky frame had become hardened by heavy work. Still, he worried!

Pierre was ever so grateful to the family of New Catholics who promised his family their warmth and hospitality. While he also was indebted for the possibility of a job, he worried how well he would hold up to these demands.

How, he asked himself, could he enforce the tyranny expected of him as a prison guard? How could he bring himself to inflict pain on the Huguenot prisoners when he had protected himself by converting? How could he ever cope with such pangs of conscience? How could he live with himself if he failed?

Part of him welcomed the slow plodding of Don-the-Donkey.

Part III

The Prison Story

La Tremblade Prison

Chapter 19

Inside La Tremblade

Today Charles couldn't get thoughts of his capture out of his mind. Months had passed since being beaten on the wharf at Place de la Coubre. It was rumored that these hoodlums had newly joined the ranks of dragoons and had to prove themselves. Huguenot ships like *L'Esprit* were their prime targets.

He tried to remember what the last moments of freedom had felt like. Then he recalled the sudden sting on the neck when a dragoon ripped off his Huguenot cross and threw it into the water. His legs were beaten so badly he couldn't walk. Unconscious, he was thrown into the cart along with two crewmen who were already dead.

It gave him some relief to focus on the Captain and crew of *L'Esprit*. Most vivid was the last night on shipboard, when the Captain named those who would be part of the crew on the voyage to America the following spring. Charles would have been among them.

Often *L'Esprit* carried Huguenots to Dover and Plymouth, England. On that particular voyage they would have only carried passengers who were headed for America. He had been told the ship could carry up to a hundred people. Presumably most of them would be Huguenots who wanted to flee.

The sailors were confident they could make the challenging trip. They were accustomed to coping with fierce storms in the English Channel and four of them had crossed the Atlantic before.

The reality of his surroundings could be blotted out only fleetingly. Reality was, that here he was in prison, at La Tremblade where men were crowded into a large open pen containing hundreds of prisoners. The building was four stories high, constructed of heavy stone and open from floor to ceiling. Sitting down, even to sleep, could mean being trampled. Sweltering hot in summer, it was bitter cold day and night during the winter. Their bare feet were numbed beyond feeling on the cold stone floors. They shared upper body heat along with lice.

Over these many months Charles had plenty of time to think. Soon after he arrived, a prisoner standing beside him collapsed and died. Being closest, he snatched the shoes off the dead man's feet. Cold as these crude wooden shoes were, it was better than being barefoot.

More than that the shoes provided him a way to keep track of time, a calendar so to speak. The sharp edge of a broken mussel shell he found lying in the courtyard, made a perfect tool to chip soft poplar. Every month after the full moon had cast a bright strip of light high on the wall, Charles chipped another tiny notch along the sole. He could already count eight.

He shuddered to think he could be there for life! How long was a life time? It could be short under these conditions. Frequent flogging of prisoners was routine. While this gave the guards plenty of exercise, the prisoners got none. In addition to floggings and lice, there were rats, inedible gruel, and a terrible stench that would remain with them forever. Already Charles thought he must have lost 40 pounds. His arm and chest muscles that had been deeply contoured from years of making sails were now flabby and flat.

One day a guard pulled Charles out of this massive cell to beat him. Then he pushed Charles into a small cell crowded with five others. Why things happened one way or another was never clear. He was totally numb from the experience. By now, he had learned not to think, to reason, nor to question.

When he was in less pain, he wondered and worried about his family back in La Rochelle, and his sister in St. Felix.

While wedged against a fellow prisoner in this tight cell, he felt a hand touch his. Shrinking in fear at first, he then felt a wad of paper. In the dark there was no way to know what all this meant. It would be days before the band of six would see daylight, on a rare foray into the courtyard.

The other prisoner stayed close. His back shielded Charles so he could safely look at this strange wad of paper. Having been tantalized by it for so long, he was delighted to see that it was from Madelaine! He read the three short lines twice before putting it in his mouth to swallow. He was glad they knew his whereabouts and were praying for him. As Madelaine had hoped, he did feel somewhat less isolated.

This note greatly puzzled Charles, however. How had his sister learned to write? The primitive French looked as though it was written by a child, yet clearly it expressed his sister's thoughts. Several days later he was moved back to the large pen.

Although he had plenty of time to think, little gave him any relief. When he was first imprisoned he had thought a great deal about the long voyage his shipmates would be making. Now, late in the spring of 1686, he wonder whether they had arrived safely.

His thoughts focused on the ship's Captain, an experienced navigator, who could read the stars like the palm of his hand. With a new compass on board he could easily locate the tip of Manhattan Island. Charles recalled hearing one of the crewmen say that of the many languages spoken there, English predominated since they had taken it over from the Dutch in 1664 and renamed the fast-growing community for their own Duke of York.

Charles reasoned that probably he would never know whether they reached New York. Many of the Huguenot passengers aboard would expect to settle, as he had hoped to do, a few miles to the north of there, in the town they had already named New Rochelle. How lucky those earlier settlers were, to have left France before their town was pillaged as Madelaine's last note indicated.

Over nearly a year, Charles had received five brief messages from Madelaine. The procedure was similar each time. There was suddenly harsher treatment, removal to the pen of six men, followed by the transfer of a wad of paper to his hand from a fellow prisoner. The contents of these letters heartened him on the one hand, but they worried and saddened him on the other.

What puzzled him most was the repeated reference to the flax crop and weaving. What, he wondered, was she trying to tell him?

Now that he had not heard from Madelaine for more than six months, Charles began to worry. Had his greatest fear become a reality? Had she too met a bad fate, illness, or injury? Had the dragoons invaded her home?

He could never have guessed that she and her family had become "New Catholics" to protect themselves the best way they could.

Tim, who had been on watch the night the men had boarded *L'Esprit* in the harbor of Place de la Coubre, was suspected of being a Huguenot too and thrown in jail.

Crowded tightly among the prisoners, he occasionally heard the French accent of Huguenots that was like that of Charles. He searched the sea of faces. One day Tim caught sight of him, but it wasn't for another several months that their eyes met.

That puzzled Charles. "Why," he wondered, "would Tim, a devout Catholic be imprisoned with all these Huguenots?" Timid as Tim was he was not one to commit a crime. Never did the two seamen have the opportunity to meet in the big pen nor in the six-man cell that Charles was transferred to at irregular intervals.

Charles would never know that his own plight was the direct result of Tim's failure to call out a warning during night watch. Nor would Charles ever hear that Tim had been called before the Captain's Mast and thrown off the ship. Neither would he have realized Tim, speechless as he was, could not explain to his captors that he was not a Huguenot.

120

On the other hand, Tim would know only too well that two shipmates had been killed and that his best friend and another faced life behind bars—all because of this drastic failure. Tim hadn't uttered a word since his capture. Not only was this a customary barometer of his stress it could have been more. His jaw had been broken by the dragoons at the end of the gangplank that morning late in August, 1685.

During those endless months Charles and Tim caught sight of each other only occasionally. Even under the best of circumstances Tim would have had a hard time conveying to Charles how terrible he felt for causing the dreadful drubbing he, Tim, had caused that day on the wharf. And, Tim would carry to his grave the guilt he felt for the deaths of the other two crewmen, despite the fact that they were the ones who had been hardest on him when he first came aboard *L'Esprit*.

Chapter 20

New Guard

Purple-gray skies hovered above the western horizon, promising a frightful July thunder storm. Pierre's hand shot up to catch his cap before a heavy gust blew it away. It was borrowed and a size too big.

Pierre looked down the long cobblestone street. Far away and deep in an apple orchard lush with fruit, there loomed a huge stone building—rigid, frigid, and fearsome.

Silhouetted against ominous skies, a row of evenly-spaced black turkey vultures screeched at him from the roofline. He tried to affirm his self-confidence by a firm stride, but his stomach belied him. It was tied in tight knots by the time he reached the door. He removed his cap, to imply his respectful intent when he applied for the job.

"Sit down," the warden barked from behind his battered old desk. "Yes, we need more guards," he said, appraising the new applicant. "You're strong. You'll do." He pushed a piece of paper across the desk for him to sign.

A flashback to writing lessons made Pierre grateful to Nicole. He looked at the quill pen laid before him. The tip looked familiar, but the one Nicole furnished had no holder such as this. He pondered how to grasp it. When he did, it felt very strange.

Since Nicole had prepared the quills for them, the ink well on the table had no significance for him. He picked up the pen. With some sense of ownership in the process, he pressed it against the paper. Nothing happened.

"Have to dip it in the ink," the warden said.

As unsettling as this stark setting was, Pierre performed

quite well. His signature was acceptable even if keeping it on the line still presented a challenge. Nicole would have been proud.

"You read?" The warden growled in cryptic tones.

With his self-confidence partially restored, Pierre replied: "Yes, I can read. That says my name, right there on that line." The warden nodded.

"Report for the night shift."

As ordered, Pierre climbed the three flights of dirty, dark, stone steps, hollowed in the pattern that heavy footsteps had laid down over the past century. Promptly at 10 that night he faced the heavy door and stood at attention as he presumed was expected. Perhaps he felt his crisp manner would offset the ill-fitting uniform provided by his family's host. A billy club and a square-cut iron key hung from his belt. Holding a lighted oil wick in one hand, he inserted the heavy key into the enormous black lock with the other. He pushed the door open ever so slowly. Hinges creaked at punctuated intervals.

He gasped. Even with the faint light of the oil wick, he could see that it opened onto a narrow catwalk. Just as frightening was the swarming sea of screaming, stinking humanity that carpeted the floor far below in the fading light of this late summer evening.

He grasped the side ropes. An electrifying response shot up

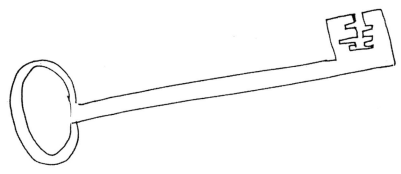

A heavy square-cut iron key to La Tremblade

his arm. In reality, Madelaine's Grandfather Germaine had no connection to the hemp rope here at La Tremblade, but he didn't have to. Its rough surface immediately placed Pierre back on the shaky ladder at church.

Terrorized, he froze. He felt faint but he knew he couldn't back down. The humiliation would be more devastating, more serious this time; another's life was involved.

A powerful feeling flooded over him: he felt he and Madelaine had weakened in their faith in stark contrast to the bulwark of strength of her predecessors. Together his faith, his mind, and his legs all seemed weak and cast their grip on him as he faced the chasm below. "I can't move!" He whispered to himself, "But how can I keep any self respect if I don't?" His love for Madelaine and the deep concern they all felt for her brother forced him to take the next step.

Pierre's heart beat harder than ever.

That first night as he stepped out onto the catwalk, there was a skinny, blonde-haired young man nearly 19 years old who was standing virtually below him. Tim looked up and stared, puzzled by the sound of the guard's voice. The accent sounded the same as his shipmate Charles. It was definitely the voice of a Huguenot, maybe even someone from La Rochelle.

How could it be that he, a Catholic in good standing, was being held because he was suspected of being a Huguenot, while the guard who held control over their lives, had a distinct Huguenot accent. "Was he was losing his mind?"

Charles heard the same voice as he stood beneath the catwalk at the other end and knew immediately whose it was! What puzzled him was that the tone and the volley of words were totally disparate and mysteriously different from anything he knew of this man. Pierre had always spoken softly and with respect to his family, especially his sister. "What on earth is going on?"

The planks of the catwalk were barely two-feet wide and

swayed with every step. The sagging hand ropes on each side were almost more than Pierre could deal with but no one could come to his rescue this time. Just the reverse, his prescribed task was to rescue another.

As dawn came up he had to make another dreaded foray onto the shaky catwalk. Partly to forge his own confidence, and partly because it was his job, he shouted out another stern message.

Charles strained to see over the heads of hundreds of other prisoners to see the face that matched this voice.

When Pierre reached the far end of the catwalk and turned, their eyes met. In a flash each of them executed disciplined distance and disinterest. Not a doubt. That was Pierre. Surely Madelaine must be near. Charles hoped for some news. Before he could contemplate this further, the new guard announced with stern clarity: "My name is Pierre Anton."

"What?" Charles could scarcely hold it in. Now he was totally confused.

The guard embarked on a verbal tirade about the flagrant sins of the prisoners, especially the Huguenots. Out in the courtyard, the new guard proceeded to flog selected individuals as a warning to others that he meant business. When he came to Charles, he was verbally and physically even more abusive. Neither chanced a hint of recognition.

A few days later, out in the courtyard, Pierre's verbal abuse of Charles escalated. New invectives were heaped on old as Charles was hauled off to be isolated in a single, dark cell where the inedible gruel was diluted even more.

After an extended time in cramped solitary confinement, his muscles pained day and night. He knew the stench would live with him forever. He felt he had already been there that long. He was still wearing the clothes he had been captured in. They were so stiff with filth, they could stand alone.

A sliver of the full moon shone through a narrow crack in the cell wall. It was time to chip another wedge into the sole of his shoe. This would be the third one he had carved while in solitary.

He sat cross-legged on the damp dirt floor that was cold even in summer. After removing his right shoe, he counted from the heel along the inner border to the toe and around the outer edge, "…22, …23." Drawing the sharp edge of his broken mussel shell against this soft wood, he carved number 24.

As the months passed and Tim had not seen Charles, he feared the worst. He would feel more guilt over what might have happened to Charles than for the certain deaths of those two other crew members. They were the ones he had heard his shipmates yelling about that dreadful morning while he was still hiding in the hold. After all, it had been Charles who had befriended him on shipboard, and defended him against those two old sailors who tormented him.

"Without my cross and my rosary beads, all the Hail Marys I say won't save me."

Tim and Charles had followed different religious faiths, but these differences had dissolved through their deep friendship, a friendship that permitted respect for the other person's religion without loss of the faith that was their own. "Surely," Tim reasoned, "the same God must hear the pleas and prayers of both."

Chapter 21

Freedom by a Thread

The gruff voice of a night guard pierced the silence along the basement cells. With a simple "*Out!*" he emptied the cell on either side as Charles steeled himself against another unexplained flogging. When the guard came to his cell he turned the rusty key and entered in silence, closing the door behind him. Charles shook, fearing the worst.

When at last he spoke, his whisper carried the humane tones of Pierre La Fountaine. Loosening the top of his uniform, he pulled out a dark brown monk's robe and whispered, "Put this on. I'll be right back. And here is a cross I made at the blacksmith's. That should give you a pass."

In an instant Madelaine's messages made sense. She was giving him his "Freedom by a thread!"

Pierre reappeared with another prisoner and doled out abuse appropriate to one being put in solitary. Charles slid out as the new prisoner was pushed inside. Pierre officiously escorted the visiting monk down the narrow hallway. Appropriate to his new role, Charles stopped briefly at other cells to bestow blessings. This allowed him a moment of silent gratitude and blessings for his brother-in-law and sister.

Pierre escorted Charles out the front door of the prison with the reverence any Catholic would have paid to a member of the cloth. He gave his brother-in-law these directions: "Walk around to the back of the prison, deep into the apple orchard. There you will find Madelaine with Don-the-Donkey and the cart." Even though Charles knew him as Don Juan, when he heard Pierre refer to him as Don-the-Donkey, his emotions cracked.

Madelaine hid him under a heavy load of straw and lifted the 18-month-old twins on top. The older children sat on either side to keep the little squirmers from climbing out. While it was a challenge to keep the youngsters quiet, it was harder for other reasons for the adult siblings to put their feelings of sadness, happiness, and relief on hold. They were so close to their goal they dared not chance discovery.

They had to go only a couple of miles to Place de la Coubre, but travel was agonizingly slow, governed by the whims of an always-reluctant donkey. Madelaine stopped the donkey on the rise overlooking the wharf that Charles recalled only too vividly. She whispered to Charles to change into Pierre's clothes in the bottom of the cart and leave his own.

Charles was more than 60 pounds lighter and so much taller, his legs would hang out. He felt something stitched inside the pant's pocket. When he recognized the wooden cross their grandfather had carved for Madelaine's confirmation, he was overwhelmed with emotion.

Changing clothes in the cramped and scratchy space of the donkey cart had its problems. After he maneuvered out of his clothes and into Pierre's, he slipped the monk's robe on to maintain a safe identity until the very last minute. Filthy as his seamen's clothes were after the past two years they were a tangible tie to her brother that Madelaine kept for some time.

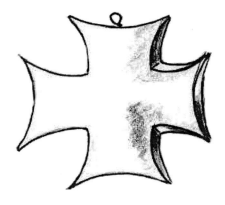

Madelaine urged the donkey onto the wharf. Still unspoken, Charles' deep appreciation to Madelaine and to Pierre for his escape was limited to a brief tearful hug when he climbed out and removed his robe for the last time. After thrusting the monk's robe into Madelaine's hands he turned toward the ship at dock. After a few steps he stopped.

Rushing back to the cart, he whispered frantically, "Madelaine, tell Pierre, to get Tim out next...." Breathlessly, he added, "He's tall, blonde, skinny, and he stutters. He's not even a Huguenot."

For a minute Madelaine wondered why Charles wanted to put a Catholic at the head of the list, until she was jolted by the fact she was one, too.

Neither Charles, Madelaine, nor Pierre had a clue about how many of "Madelaine's Monks" Don-the-Donkey would carry over the next few years to ships when they docked at Place de la Coubre.

Nor would they ever know it was all because of Tim's severe stutter that the ongoing series of tragic events had doomed the crewmen of *L'Esprit* of both Huguenot and Catholic faiths.

With so many little hands to hold onto in the dark, it was not until Madelaine had turned the donkey cart around, that she realized Joseph was missing. Then she heard a faint cry from Charles on the wharf. "He's here with me."

Charles carried Joseph back and lifted him into the cart. After he gave his sister a quick kiss he crossed the uneven planks again. The ship waiting there would cast off at high tide. This wasn't *L'Esprit* but the same spirit of the crew was evident to Charles.

Charles inhaled the clear salt air. He was on his way to America at last. He had nothing to carry with him but his indomitable faith, the desire to practice it in freedom, and the Huguenot cross that would forever be a link to his sister and the memory of their grandfather.

Lineage of Charles Germaine

Documents show that Charles Germaine was a fugitive from La Tremblade prison in 1687, two years after the Edict of Nantes had been revoked.

Relevant lineage of Charles Germaine follows. The name is also spelled Germond, German, and Jarmin.

He had six children:
> Margaret, married Paix Cassaneau
> Mary, married Andre Sigourney 2nd
> Charles Jr.
> Ober
> Peter
> Isaac German moved to Dutchess County on, or before,
>   1736 and married. He died in 1763.

His children were:
> Isaac Jr. who married in 1736 to Catherine Haff.
> Susanne, married in 1736 to Lawrence Haff.

James	died, 1788.
Peter baptized	November 6, 1760.[1]
Seaman "	November 6, 1760.
Phebe "	November 6, 1760.
Deborah "	November 6, 1760.
Sarah "	November 6, 1760, married Jonathan Vincent.[2]

Sarah Germond,[3] was born July 10, 1760 and died November 22, 1795 at the age of 35. She married Jonathan Vincent on October 1, 1780.

They had 6 children; the 6th was Gilbert Issac, who had 13 children and the 5th of that generation was Jonathan Vincent. He was the grandfather of Mary Vincent who married Jonathan Ham.

They had 5 children, the oldest of whom was my grandfather, Eugene Ham. Their oldest child of 6 was my mother, Mary Ham.

I am the end of this line, the 10th documented generation of the Huguenot fugitive of La Tremblade Prison, Charles Germaine, who fled in 1687.[4]

---

1   It was common practice then to have the children of various ages all baptized at one time, when the traveling pastor was available.

2   See *The Vincent Family, Descendants of Adrian Vincent*, Millbrook Press, Millbrook, New York 1959.

3   Great-grand-daughter of Charles Germaine.

4   February 21, 1976 I married Harry Beskind, MD in Princeton, New Jersey. I have two step-sons, Mark and Daniel. On June 16, 1994, my husband and I were divorced.

Chronology

Bold indicates factual history
Italics defines fictional aspects.

1509 – John Calvin was born

1536 – Calvin wrote "Christianae religionis Institutio"

1564 – Calvin died

1572 – Massacre of St. Bartholomew in Paris killed 2000 Huguenot followers and leaders.

1598 – Edict of Nantes granted freedom for Huguenots to worship

1626 – Peace of La Rochelle

1680 – Madelaine Germaine married Pierre La Fountaine in La Rochelle

1681 – son Jacques was born to Madelaine and Pierre

1683 – daughter Jeanette was born to Madelaine and Pierre

1685 – Edict of Nantes was revoked

1685 – Charles Germaine was captured and imprisoned at La Tremblade Prison

1686 – twins Mary and Joseph were born

1687 – Charles Germaine became a Huguenot fugitive from La Tremblade Prison in France

1687 – Charles Germaine landed in Boston and settled in the town of New Orford before moving a decade later to New Rochelle (NY)

An Ancestor of Mine

There was a fugitive named Charles Germaine,
an ancestor of mine who fled the iron chains
of La Tremblade Prison, in 1687,
south of his home in La Rochelle, hotbed
of Huguenot resistance, loyal Calvinists led.

His escape can be seen from two
diametrically opposed points of view.
While the Papists condemned this as a dastardly act,
the Calvinists lauded it as a daring feat,
so their religious beliefs might remain intact.

In America, Charles settled northward
of Boston in a village named New Orford.
A decade later he moved again, to join
other Huguenots from the French shoreline.
It comes as no surprise,
you can readily foretell,
they proudly named their spot
near the Hudson, New Rochelle.

2006

About the author

Barbara Knickerbocker (Beskind) was born in Washington, D.C., but grew up in the Hudson River Valley, at Bangall, New York, near Poughkeepsie and Hyde Park. She graduated from Green Mountain Junior College in 1943, and from Syracuse University in 1945 before going on to the Milwaukee–Downer College for Women to take her training for occupational therapy.

Her professional career spanned 46 years, the first 20 of which she was commissioned in the Army Medical Specialist Corps, serving in Army hospitals in the U.S. and overseas, as well as being Asst. Director of the Army School of Occupational Therapy at Fort Sam Houston, Texas.

After retiring as a major, she established the first free-standing private practice in occupational therapy in the United States, treating children and adults with learning disabilities. Her textbook on this subject was published in 1980 and has been used world-wide in English-speaking curricula.

Barbara, a writer of long standing, began yet another career, launching the BKB Press in the spring of 2008. *Powder Keg*, the first book in a trilogy of "windows on history," was published in May, 2008. It is an historical autobiography of her life and the role of distant ancestors in history.

Touches of Life in Time and Space is the second "window on history." It is a book of 40 poems and more than 50 pieces of her art work that relate to these poems. They range from historical content to her personal life experience, and an interest in Russian art.

Flax to Freedom is the third in this series of "windows on history."

BKB Press plans to publish the author's next book, *Touches of Art and the Impact of the Russian Avant-garde* in 2010. It details the history of this movement and specific artists who were instrumental in promoting it. Illustrations in *Flax to Freedom* are done in the abstract, in the style of several prominent artists of the Russian avant-garde, Varvara Stepanova in particular.

133

Breinigsville, PA USA
18 August 2009
222469BV00004B/6/P